THE REALLY

Whole Food

❖ COOKBOOK ❖

THE REALLY

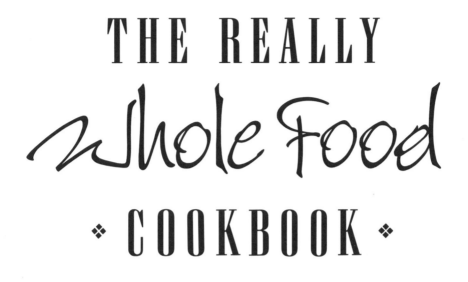

whole food

❖ COOKBOOK ❖

Food Choices
for a Sustainable Future

Dan Jason & Dawn Penny Brooks

Harbour Publishing

HARBOUR PUBLISHING
P.O. Box 219
Madeira Park, BC Canada V0N 2H0

Cover and page design by Gaye Hammond
Drawings by Gaye Hammond
Cover photograph by Richard Fukuhara/West
  Light, courtesy of Tony Stone Images
Author photograph by Mike Gluss
Page composition by The Vancouver Desktop
  Publishing Centre

Printed and bound in Canada

Canadian Cataloguing in Publication Data

Jason, Dan.
  The really whole food cookbook

  Includes index.
  ISBN 1-55017-117-8
  1. Cookery (Natural foods) 2. Vegetarian cookery.
I. Brooks, Dawn, 1950- II. Title.
TX741.J37 1994   641.5'636   C94-910754-9

Dedication

At a time when food security and safety have never been more threatened, we dedicate this book to the children who will inherit this precious Earth, and to the increasing numbers of growers who are sowing and saving heritage seeds.

Acknowledgements

We would like to thank the following friends and customers who have contributed recipes to this cookbook: Diane Quittenton, Martha Warde, Margaret Williams, Carlos Beca, Gwen Mallard, Ted Rhodes, Kevin Aguanno.

Thanks also to the following friends for their longtime inspiration in preparing whole foods well: Randy Hooper and Linda Dares, Charlie and Judy Eagle, Phyllis and Mathew Coleman, Stephen Berry and Connie Addario, and the Salt Spring Centre cooks.

Table of Contents

A Word from Dan

Whole foods are very special to me, because I learned about cooking them in a unique way. As the owner of Salt Spring Seeds, a seed company that specializes in beans and grains, I've grown and tasted many hundreds of varieties from around the world. The more I try, the more enthusiastic I become about really whole foods.

My career as an ardent gardener began in the early 1980s when the acreage across the road from me on Salt Spring Island (one of BC's Gulf Islands) was purchased by a group of "off-islanders." The land quickly came to be called the Salt Spring Centre, a fitting name for a yoga, retreat and meditation facility in the heart of the island.

Thanks to a synchronicity of time, place and people, I soon became the Centre's head gardener. Two acres of rich bottom land and a budget that enabled me to purchase seeds, supplies and equipment provided a challenging opportunity to grow food for large numbers of people. Our meals were vegetarian, so I researched and grew crops that were high-protein foods capable of rounding out a diet rich in fruits and vegetables.

My first major discovery was a soybean called Black Jet that matured easily in the growing conditions at the Centre. Till then, I'd had disappointing experiences cooking whole soybeans. The Black Jets, though, tasted good with minimal seasoning and caused no gas or indigestion for me or others. At the same time, I grew varieties of pinto, chili, soup and baking beans that were more delicious than any I had purchased from stores.

I was not only trying out various beans but also testing grains that would be appropriate for a kitchen garden. Two crops that stood out hail from South America. Amaranth and quinoa are gorgeous, drought-tolerant plants with a high yield that make very filling and satisfying meals.

When I started Salt Spring Seeds in 1988, listing some of my beans and grains in a mail order seed catalogue, I felt I was really onto something. North Americans were beginning to shift to a more plant-based diet, yet our growing habits had not caught up. For example, billions of bushels of soybeans are grown annually for export, animal feed or processing, but hardly any are grown for direct human consumption.

Indeed, I was in the right place at the right time. Business has doubled yearly and my seeds are finding their way around the globe. Amaranth and quinoa have become commercial crops in Canada. Recipes for them and other "new" protein-rich plants have become standard in vegetarian cookbooks. Black Jet soybeans were recently featured in a national gardening magazine.

Soybeans, quinoa, beans and amaranth made for plenty of inspiration, but I also discovered lentils, favas, chick-peas, wheat, peas and barley. All are grown on a large scale in North America but mostly for processing into food products or for export elsewhere. This seemed amazing to me since many of these varieties are delicious cooked just as they are—simple, whole foods. Multiple revelations made my garden harvests sparkle with newness: there are pea cultivars that make fine soup peas and don't have to be split; there are barleys with hulls that are easy to rub off and are well worth cultivating for kitchen use; there are old wheat varieties, like kamut and spelt, that many people with wheat allergies can tolerate.

These discoveries I made year after year revealed three bottom-line facts about beans and grains that have remained consistent.

1. They are very easy to grow. I'm definitely convinced on this one. I've matured hundreds of varieties in cool coastal conditions, have grown them without fertilizers or irrigation and have had no serious disease or pest problems.
2. They can produce a lot of food in a small area. Ah, yes, remembering all my bountiful harvests from the Salt Spring Centre and from Mansell Farm, where I now garden.
3. They offer an incredible diversity of tastes and textures. The recipes in this cookbook are designed to show off the rich, diverse culinary possibilities in all really whole foods, especially grains and beans.

Is it a big challenge to keep enough variety in a diet that relies on beans and grains? Absolutely not! There are many easy and interesting ways to prepare beans and grains. Like most North American kids, I grew up on a meat and dairy diet. It's been a gradual transition for me to so-called fibre foods, finding out over many years that they needn't be bland or boring. It's all a matter of habit—my three kids have never eaten much meat or dairy food and so have never

developed an addicted appetite for them.

There have been a lot of hurdles for me to leap over along the way. For instance, when Frances Moore Lappé emphasized in *Diet for a Small Planet* the need to practice protein combinations, it made bean and grain preparation seem too serious and academic—daunting, even. (Later, in a revised version, she concurred with other authorities that we don't need the same complex of nutrition in every meal we eat.) Another thing that put me off were the horrible-tasting soybean varieties that were available back in the early '70s. Grown for animal feed, they were enough to put one off soybeans forever!

Through the '70s and '80s my diet came to consist of foods such as tofu, brown rice, whole grain bread, soy milk and lots of fresh fruit and vegetables. I found my vitality was improving immensely and I was missing cheese and meat less and less. But it wasn't until I discovered the likes of Black Jet soybeans and embarked on Salt Spring seeds that I discovered the potential in cooking unadulterated whole foods. Cooking them and receiving enthusiastic responses from my friends and family has inspired my own enthusiasm, and the joy continues!

Is it a lot of trouble to cook with whole foods? On the contrary. It is a simple activity that is refreshing and liberating. I don't have to deal with batters, doughs or fancy ingredients. The simplicity of whole foods calls for simple additions. Cooking beans and grains involves simmering them until they're done. Then it's a straightforward matter of adding dressings, sauces or sautés, or even enjoying their unadorned wholeness. Nor do I have to mess with greasy pans or packaging that deceptively identifies itself as "Part of a Simple Lifestyle."

The rich variety of grains and beans that awaits discovery by North Americans is exciting for many more reasons than their easy preparation. Soybeans and chick-peas, favas and peas, wheat and lentils, amaranth and quinoa come in all manner of sizes, shapes, colours, tastes and textures. Twenty years ago I knew and appreciated dozens of cheeses, wines and cuts of meat, but never thought to expect the diverse, delightful and delectable surprises I've had from beans and grains. Like any delicacy, they have more or less flavour or texture. But my, there are some yummy ones!

My trip to Ethiopia in the winter of 1993 greatly broadened my perspective on whole foods. I was sponsored by the Unitarian Service Committee of Canada to observe first-hand an agricultural program called Seeds of Survival. Scientists and farmers are working together to bring back some of the old crops that were almost lost during the period of drought and civil war in the mid-1980s. Ethiopians have farmed their land for as long as anyone on this earth, and over 80 percent of them are still farmers. Certain that their crops are better than modern hybrids, they are extremely happy to be growing them again.

What amazed me was that the Ethiopians grow many of the foods featured in this cookbook, including favas, lentils, chick-peas, barley, wheat, beans, peas and amaranth. Their farms are similar in scope to the three acres I work here at Mansell Farm, and each acreage provides enough food to feed a large extended family. I was also struck by the vibrant health of both the Ethiopian people and their agricultural land, dispelling the false expectations our media had tattooed in my mind.

I returned to Mansell Farm with a vision of 20 percent of North Americans growing their own food instead of the 2 percent who do now. That vision persists. Growing food is a wonderful vocation that works best when people maintain intimacy with what they cultivate. The large-scale, high-input agriculture that is practised in North America has only worked because there was lots of good soil around when it began. But factor in all the costs of corporate farming and it is clearly not sustainable. Our soil and water are already so depleted and polluted, there is precious little time to turn things around. To grow foods such as those featured in this cookbook using methods that improve rather than impede the land's health, and on a scale that can provide for our own needs, is to my mind the way to go.

One further aspect I consider crucial is our attitude toward seeds themselves. Modern agriculture must learn to appreciate heritage seeds, as the Ethiopians and all traditional farmers do. As fish stocks dwindle to zero and meat products are increasingly laced with hormones and biocides, our safest, most sustainable food choices become beans and grains. They are not only whole foods. As seeds they represent a living legacy bequeathed to us by countless generations of farmers living with, rather than against, the earth. Corporate agriculture's current path, trying to take over nature's job by producing seeds in the laboratory is, I think, both dangerous and unnecessary. The highest quality food crops already exist and await our discovery and appreciation.

The notion of eating whole grains and beans is not such a radical one when you remember that such fare has sustained countless cultures all over the globe. As few as two or three of these foods have formed the staple diets of huge groups of people. We now have the opportunity to enjoy a great many of them, and to celebrate a diet unprecedented in health-bestowing diversity. Beans and grains can help us to restore (and re-inhabit) our land and create a sustainable relationship with it. What's more, they're simply great food!

Happy cooking!

—Dan Jason

A Word from Dawn

My background as a musician, educator, author and editor has hardly prepared me to collaborate on a whole foods cookbook. Before moving to Salt Spring Island, my active, single, urban "career" life found me eating in restaurants frequently, cooking mostly for myself and sometimes for housemates. But even then a day off usually found me in the kitchen, and one of my favourite social events was to prepare and share a meal with friends. Cooking has been a part of my life since I was a child, and has always been a cherished pastime.

Cooking grains and beans has been a relatively recent discovery for me. All my life I was encouraged to appreciate diverse foods, but I grew up on standard meat and potato fare with a maritime influence. Like many women, my early relationship with food was somewhat of a love/hate affair. After years of trying "diets" to lose weight and falling off into compulsive binges, I finally decided in my late twenties that my attitude to food needed a nudge. Ultimately, my greatest success in both losing and maintaining my weight came from eating only when my body registered hunger, slowly and in moderation. Instead of depriving myself, which diets meant to me back then, I became more fully conscious of why and how I was eating.

Several years later, health problems forced me to consider more seriously what I was eating. I found it hard to believe that the headaches I was experiencing at the time could be related to my bowel, but a health crisis ensued that convinced me my doctor was right. I followed her advice to eat less meat and dairy products and cleanse my system with herbal teas and juice fasts. However, old habits die hard. I was not enthralled by tofu or tempeh, nor was I inclined to explore other packaged "health" foods or rummage through bulk bins of grains and legumes I didn't know how to prepare. Besides, the demands of my career, which often included travel and excruciating deadlines, and the fact that I had no family to prepare meals for, made easy excuses to put off further exploration in favour of old standbys.

So five years ago, when I moved from Toronto to Salt Spring Island, my whole food cooking repertoire was limited to brown rice, split peas, kidney and navy beans. I had no idea what a farm-fresh egg tasted like, let alone veggies straight from my own garden! Rarely had my hands been in the soil since my mudpie days. Never had I lived in such a beautiful place, or noticed how my food choices affected the natural environment. I was learning more about ecological issues and was amazed at the extent to which modern agriculture threatens human and environmental health. I had not realized the abuse to which feedlot animals are subjected. I'd never eaten organic foods or free-range eggs, poultry or meat.

My first year here changed all that. My partner Gary and I moved into a home with a garden—a daunting prospect given our lack of gardening experience. Enter Dan, with whose generous help—partly in exchange for some work I did on his book *Greening the Garden*—the herb garden I'd always wanted and a generous vegetable garden became realities. The following spring brought the delights of fresh-picked, untreated food. The first spinach, potatoes, tomatoes and corn we harvested brought back childhood memories of staying at my Aunt Flo's farm cottage, where I'd first tasted food fresh from the garden. Never since had vegetables tasted *so* good! What a revelation. And what a delight to find that everything in the garden yielded a plentiful harvest, despite the intermittent care we gave it.

Working on *Greening the Garden* was not only pleasurable for me, but enlightening. It opened my eyes to an array of foods and medicines I'd never heard of, to the importance of organic, sustainable agriculture from an ecological perspective, and to the political implications of my food choices. Like Dan, other friends I met on the island that year impressed me with their love for plants, their desire to share their knowledge about diverse gardens and to sustain their families in the process. Island potlucks broadened my experience of vegetarian fare and gave me a hint of what "community" is about. The knowledge I gained and the caring I experienced had profound effects on my buying habits and food choices by the end of year one. I'd also experienced first-hand the joys of tending a garden.

That same year, I also decided to help Gary develop an alternative radio station. It was a worthwhile venture that I enjoyed, but it took us off island frequently and stretched our resources. My energy was pulled in every direction, juggling business, house, yard and garden work, entertaining business colleagues and personal study.

Finally, in year two, a car accident forced me to recognize that what I had come to Salt Spring for and what I was creating did not jibe. I was off-balance. Gary and I had moved here to change our diet, simplify our lifestyle and become part of a community in a way our city life had seemed to defy. Instead, I had become involved in a "cause" that brought out my workaholic tendencies, kept me entrenched in old patterns and prevented me from setting roots. It was like an addiction in itself.

These realizations led to the end of my marriage and my work on the project. Both of them are part of who I am now, but I could not continue working toward an external, future possibility to the exclusion of caring for my own garden and my own health, in the present.

After a period of healing, a mix of circumstances led to my move to Mansell Farm last year. Now, in helping Dan at Salt Spring Seeds, I plant, tend, preserve, photograph, taste test, cook and package an incredible diversity of grains, legumes, flowers and garlic. And having cooked and tasted well over a hundred different kinds of beans—and several dozen grains—I find myself collaborating on this book! All but a few of the recipes are Dan's, and while I haven't tried cooking all of them myself, knowing Dan's day-to-day cooking as I do I have no reason to question the rave reviews he's received from customers!

In my own process of discovery I've let go of three misconceptions I once had about these foods: that they're bland (translation: boring), that they call for special ingredi-

ents, and that they need lots of preparation time. A whole food diet need never be boring. I have been known in the past for my love of wine, and I've tasted many a cheese along with it. I now realize that beans offer as rich a variety of bouquet, texture, flavour and aftertaste—with far more nourishment than my former addictions! And while "vegetarian" cookbooks once seemed daunting to me for all the ingredients that weren't on my kitchen shelf, most of these recipes call for things you're likely to have. Soaking and cooking the beans needs a bit of forethought, but then they only require quick and simple additions. Even the soaking and cooking can be easier, if you do an occasional "mass" cooking for a few days' meals.

I can also recommend growing some of your own food. My experience as a gardener continues to expand—I've followed the plants featured in this book through one whole cycle now, having planted my first field of beans last spring! They have been abundant and easy to maintain, despite this year's hot weather and lack of rain. More important, they are a pleasure to live with. They have such stable, vital energy that just walking through the garden gives me a lift.

My city life gave me little opportunity to gain this kind of direct experience of the earth and the sources of my food—living plants and animals. Living here, with the pleasures of natural beauty and the garden, is an inspiration. It helps me to stay in touch with my own rhythm. It inspires me to become a human "being" instead of a human "doing." Thankfully, my old worries about making a living are gradually giving way to simply living.

When it comes to food choices, the combination of modern agriculture, media advertising and urban living makes it difficult to find an appropriate middle ground between quick packaged foods and whole foods; between choosing to become vegetarian or eating more meat; between the convenience of fast food and the very different rhythms of tending a garden. Wendell Berry asks: What are people for? Has the influence of modern agriculture, forcing people from the land to urban centres in a short period of time, truly brought added meaning or enrichment to our lives?

Working with Salt Spring Seeds, I'm heartened by the evidence I see that more and more people are growing their own food and living closer to the land. I'm awed at the potential there is in people growing their own food and/or making food choices with conscience. Since food is our most intimate connection to nature, and a priority in our daily lives, I can't help but think that we billions of food lovers, cooks and caregivers who make decisions about food many times a day can create a powerful demand for untreated, locally grown food. When we put food choices and secure food supply at the top of our list of priorities, our quality of life will improve. What's more, at a time when disposable incomes are shrinking, beans and grains are the best investment we can make in terms of nutritional value and energy savings.

Bringing this book to you has been a great pleasure. I do hope you enjoy using it as much as I have enjoyed co-creating it!

—Dawn Brooks

About this Book

North Americans now recognize the importance of fibre in the diet, and whole grains and legumes, nuts and seeds are widely accepted antidotes to the standard, overly refined Western diet. We hope this cookbook both provides information and corrects popular misconceptions about the foods themselves as well as preparing them. It offers a wide range of recipes featuring legumes and grains in their most simple, whole state, along with a few of our favourite garlic dishes. All are substantially nutritious and fill the need for a high-fibre, low-fat diet, and most require minimal preparation. We find that whole foods, in their utter simplicity, need only a few added ingredients that most people have in their kitchens. A few recipes call for dairy products, but none of them require meat.

The book is right for you if you

- want to include whole, plant-based foods in your family's diet;

- want to reduce your reliance on meat-based dishes and chemically treated foods;

- are a gardener who wants to expand or start growing food crops;

- want to make new food choices for personal, family or environmental health.

Though vast numbers of legumes and grains are available for use in North America, we tend to grow these foods for export, or as animal feed. Our agriculture system favours beef and dairy farming over horticultural concerns. As a result, we often import these products when we could be growing them ourselves. We process and package them, then transport them thousands of miles and end up paying not only a high end-cost as consumers, but the hidden environmental and health costs of these energy-intensive processes as taxpayers.

Why *Really* Whole Food?

Research shows that processing food in any way causes nutrition to be lost. Besides the cost to our health, processing, packaging and transporting foods is energy-intensive, and costly to the environment. So this cookbook doesn't give directions for cooking with tempeh or tofu, or making bread from spelt or kamut flour, or using other ingredients that are derived from the original, whole food. It is about incorporating some of the most delicious, nourishing whole foods we have on this planet into our diets easily. For example, grains and legumes have been a traditional pair in diets around the world for well over 10,000 years. As the seeds of living plants, eaten raw or simply dried, nothing could be closer to whole food than these.

Why *Sustainable* Food Choices?

It feels wonderful to have an answer to that most crucial question: "How can we all live sustainably on this planet?" We're not saying that whole foods are *the* answer. But our experience growing and eating the foods in this cookbook has convinced us that they could provide everybody on this planet with a healthy diet, at only a fraction of the environmental costs now incurred by "modern" agriculture.

The popularity of a plant-based diet is increasing dramatically. More and more people are re-thinking their food choices for a variety of reasons. Masses of people on this continent depend on food, care about its quality, and want to ensure a secure supply for everyone's needs. Even small dietary changes, for example reducing refined and meat-based foods by a modest 10 percent, can add up to incredible benefits when multiplied by the millions of people living in North America. The differences that are already occurring are starting to reveal possibilities of a new and glorious Garden, a greener Earth.

The Ingredients

But where is one to find some of the ingredients called for in this cookbook?

You can start by learning about beans and grains. Check the Helpful Resources and Further Reading section in this book (p. 196), and browse through the many books about the health and environmental benefits of a bean- and grain-oriented diet. Dan's *Greening the Garden: A Guide to Sustainable Growing* (New Society Publishers, 1991) is a good place to start.

We encourage you to familiarize yourself with local community sources of grains and legumes, preferably untreated and grown according to organic standards. Some of the varieties available in health food stores or bulk bins of supermarkets are quite good tasting. If stores, wholesalers or farmers near you don't yet carry whole beans and grains, you can encourage them to do so by asking for them.

Like anything else, beans and grains deteriorate with age, only the process is slower and less noticeable. Recently harvested dry beans will have bright rich col-

ours. Both grains and beans are more digestible and cook up quicker than those transported thousands of miles and stored for months or years. To find out, check with your supplier.

Dietitians and other health practitioners are starting to form alliances with growers keen on getting whole, healthful food to people. Seed companies are beginning to list beans and grains in their catalogues and many stores are starting to feature them. Farmer/consumer relationships that eliminate middle people are now cropping up all over the continent: in "community shared agriculture," for example, people advance money to local growers in return for regular harvest pick-up or delivery. Some of these initiatives may already have started in your own area (see What You Can Do, p. 201).

Let's Begin!

Until you actually cook up a variety of beans and grains from different sources, you won't know how fresh and tasty they are. Get some samples and try a taste test using the Naked Bean recipe (p. 35), in Whole Food Cooking: The Basics. We follow that with a few bean recipes, then give the basics on grains as well. On page 29 you'll find Recommended Kitchen Staples, a list of seasonings and herbs we can't live without, plus recipe ingredients that may not be as familiar to you. Many of them are now available in supermarkets as well as health and natural food stores.

We have arranged the rest of the sections in a conventional way—soups, salads, main dishes, etc.—but remember, virtually any dish that contains whole food may serve as a "main dish." Most any selection, together with a serving of bread and a simple salad, makes a wholesome, satisfying and nutritionally sound meal. The choices and combinations are endless.

We hope the special tips and techniques included throughout the text will help you in the kitchen or add to your pleasure as you're waiting for the pot to boil! And watch for the Variations and Notes. Each one refers directly to a given recipe.

You'll find background information about dietary choices and key ingredients under the heading Did You Know . . . ? Grower's Delight offers some inspiration if you're growing some of your own food, or thinking about it.

Though this is not a "why become vegetarian" or "how to change your diet" book, if you are considering such a switch, or are in transition, the Sound Nutrition notes offer nutritional information about ingredients, and tips from our own experience.

We hope that the Soul Food ssections will inspire mindfulness and respect for the food and the resources that support it. Our own observations and the quotes included in Food for Thought give additional background and insights into modern agricultural practice and its ecological implications. The quotations are from a range of people whose work in agriculture, food systems, ecology or the peace movement we admire and respect.

Additional Information

You'll find this information following the recipes:

- Sources.

- Helpful Resources and Further Reading: books that have inspired or informed us about food and cooking, as well as names and addresses of organizations that are doing positive work in this direction.

- What You Can Do: food choices for a sustainable household and for a sustainable community.

- Guide for Growers: a short guide to growing your own beans and grains.

- Index of recipes.

We hope you have as much pleasure cooking nature's food as we do. Bon appétit!

Whole Food Cooking: The Basics

To get you started, this section offers a guide to ingredients, cooking tips and a few simple recipes using various legumes, grains and garlic. Before trying the recipes, you may want to go on an expedition to explore local food sources. Many commercial supermarkets now carry a good selection of dried legumes in bulk food sections, including:

Brown and Red Lentils
Black-Eyed Peas
Chick-peas or Garbanzos
Great Northern Beans
Small Red Chile Beans
Black Turtle Beans
Split Green and Yellow Peas
Whole Green Peas
Baby and Large Lima Beans
Small White Navy Beans
Pinto Beans
Kidney Beans

Whole grains are harder to find, amaranth being the only choice in our local supermarket, as well as pearl and pot barley, which are both refined forms of barley and not nearly as satisfying as the whole grain.

The Recipes

Recommended Kitchen Staples

Besides the whole grains and beans, most of the ingredients called for in our recipes are foods you probably have in the kitchen, or they are easy to find at the local supermarket. Here is a list of our preferences, and a brief guide to those that may not be so familiar. You may have to look for a few of these in health or natural food stores.

Salt. We keep sea salt, vegetable salt and *gomasio*—a blend of sea salt and sesame seeds—for additions at the table.

Yeasts. Both brewer's yeast and nutritional yeast are excellent and concentrated nutritional supplements. Nutritional yeast is flavourful, often either nutty or cheeselike depending on the variety, so it can also be used as a condiment and a non-dairy substitute for Parmesan cheese.

Soy sauce. We use natural soy sauce—tamari or shoyu—which contains enzymes to aid digestion and promote healthy bacteria cultures in the intestine. Mass-produced commercial varieties are stripped of flavour and some nutrition, plus contain chemicals and colouring agents.

Vinegars. We like to have apple cider, white and red wine plus rice vinegars on hand. Rice vinegar is really special—fragrant, and slightly sweet.

Fats or Oils. Fats are healthful, concentrated energy sources but should be taken in moderation as the body stores fat and the liver actually manufactures all the cholesterol the body needs. While most of us have several tablespoons of fat a day, some experts claim we only need one!

Saturated fats in meat, butter, cheese and

other dairy products raise blood cholesterol and should be used sparingly. We prefer unsalted butter. Our absolute favourite oil for beans and grains is unrefined flax seed oil for its flavour and texture. We just drizzle it over our meal after cooking. Though it's relatively expensive and needs refrigeration, it is well known in health circles for its restorative powers. In fact, evidence suggests it helps decrease the risk of arthritis, cancer and heart disease. For more about this, ask for the booklet "Flax Oil as a True Aid against Arthritis, Heart Infarction, Cancer and Other Diseases," by Dr. Johanna Budwig, at your health food store.

We also keep extra virgin olive oil and safflower oil on hand, both cold-pressed, or less processed than other oils. These are polyunsaturated and monounsaturated oils, respectively, both of which are known to actually help lower overall blood cholesterol.

Unless a certain oil is called for in a recipe, use olive oil for salads, and canola or safflower oil for stir-frys and other heated dishes.

Herbs and Spices. Blessed with an extensive herb garden and greenhouse, we have fresh herbs all summer and dry what we need for the winter. Most herbs are easy to grow, even in containers if you don't have space for a garden, and some do well inside. Do yourself a favour and try growing a few of your favourites. The rewards are worth it!

Herbs You Can Grow Yourself

basil	garlic
bay leaves	mint
cayenne pepper	oregano
chives	parsley

Note

Cilantro is the leaves and coriander the seeds from the same plant. Coriander seeds are available commercially, but cilantro loses most of its unique flavour in drying, so it's fresh or not at all! The flavour is unusual, but once you're used to it you'll find it enlivens many bean dishes and works well in salads too. Start with a little, and increase to taste!

Note

Though dried ginger is fine for baked goods, we specify fresh grated ginger root in most recipes. It's available in most supermarkets and can be kept in the freezer for extended storage.

Sound Nutrition

Many foods besides beans and dark green leafy vegetables contain calcium in natural form that is easy to digest: nuts, sea vegetables and tahini among them.

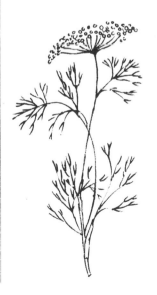

cilantro/coriander
daikon radish
dill weed and seed
fennel seed

rosemary
sage
tarragon
thyme

Spices from the Store

cardamon
chili powder
cinnamon
cloves
cumin
curry powder

ginger
nutmeg
paprika
peppercorns
saffron
turmeric

Nuts and Seeds. Due to their high fat content, nuts and seeds should be used in moderation, but they are an invaluable addition to meatless diets. They are a particularly good complement to grain dishes—nut butter on bread, nuts with pasta or as a topping on a grain pilaf. We generally buy unsalted varieties for any use. Unless used quickly, nuts and nut butters should be refrigerated to prevent rancidity.

We usually keep at least one type of dried nut on hand, usually almonds or pecans, plus one or two nut butters: peanut, almond or cashew.

As for seeds, sunflower and sesame are the most common in our kitchen, and we generally keep tahini (sesame paste) on hand. To use tahini, stir well to mix the oil and solids, then dilute a tablespoon or two with an equal amount of water to add to stir-fried vegetables or cooked grains.

Sea Vegetables. Sea vegetables are among the most nutritious foods available on the planet. They provide an abundance of vitamins, minerals and trace elements. Most notably, they contain vitamin B12, important for vegans (those who refrain from eating all meat, eggs and dairy products). As sea vegetables are so high in sodium, limit their use or avoid them if you are concerned about salt intake.

Sea vegetables are most commonly sold in sealed cellophane packages and "shake-on" containers. Available in natural food stores, they'll keep up to 2 years if sealed well and stored in a dry place.

We like to have a shaker of kelp flakes and at least one variety of dried seaweed—dulse, kombu, nori or wakame—available. Add a strip or sheet to soups or stews as they cook for added nutrition and flavour.

Soy Foods. Miso, made from fermented and aged soy, rice or barley (with salt and water), is a staple in Japanese and Chinese cooking. Within each type are a range of flavour variations, all earthy, pungently salty and with a texture similar to peanut butter. We generally add miso to soups or bean dishes. Dissolve about a tablespoon of miso in enough warm water to pour in just before cooking is complete. Add more to taste. It can also be used in sauces, dressings and dips. Usually available in plastic tubs, miso should be sealed well and keeps refrigerated for up to several months. "Quick" misos contain additives and preservatives which we avoid.

Tofu, or bean curd, is another staple in Japanese and Chinese cooking. Available in firm, soft or medium hard textures, it is sold fresh in pound or half-pound blocks immersed in water. It is packaged in plastic tubs, but many health food stores or Oriental groceries also carry it fresh in a vat of water. For the latter, make sure that the water looks fairly clean and clear, otherwise it's not likely fresh. Most tofu should be used within a week or by the date stamped on the package. Keep it immersed in water in the fridge and change the water daily.

If you are concerned about cholesterol in mayonnaise, ask for tofu mayonnaise at health or natural food stores. Soy-based cheeses are also available, even at supermarkets. In baked dishes the difference is hardly perceptible.

Legumes

Dried beans and peas, the fruits of leguminous plants, come in a vast array of colours, shapes and sizes. Cooked, they are delicious in a wide variety of main and side dishes. They are a nourishing, versatile staple, each kind with its own flavour and texture. Cooked legumes can be added to everything from soup to stews, pizzas to salads, casseroles to vegetables. They can be mashed with potatoes or squash, formed into burgers or puréed as baby food.

The Taste Test

You just can't appreciate the diversity of legumes until you've tasted several at one sitting, so do a taste test. We try four varieties at a time, if only due to the limited number of burners on the stove! Buy $1/4$ to $1/2$ cup of each variety you want to test. The amount depends on the number of "tasters"—and whether or not you're following the test with one of these recipes! To keep track of the names, we label and soak each bean variety in a glass or small dish. During cooking, we place the containers beside the appropriate burner, then spoon the beans back into them for the test. In tasting a new variety, or comparing several, we like them "naked" for a true reading. We pass the dish back and forth, each savouring a mouthful well before sharing our response. Make some notes on the varieties you like the most. (We don't mind if you write their names right in this book.) Our own descriptions for legumes we grow and test indicate the variety of tastes and textures available in the bean world:

nutty	light	creamy
substantial	robust	chewy
sweet	musky	hearty
bland	mealy	firm
gooey	tough	buttery
dry	crunchy	potato-
beany	chocolatey	like

A Word about Flatulence

We are most definitely creatures of habit, and in this culture we have grown accustomed to eating on the run. Perhaps the simplest advice we can give about the gas factor in beans is to slow down, chew longer and give the digestive process a proper start. Be sure not to ingest soaking water (but house plants like it!), and if any difficulty persists, avoid liquids till at least 15 minutes after your meal. The other antidote is to grow your own beans—recently harvested ones are easier to digest and far superior nutritionally to the bulk bin varieties.

Grower's Delight

To avoid the soaking process, try harvesting and freezing beans before the pods start to dry, at "horticultural" or "shell" stage. Simply bring water to a boil and add the frozen beans. Simmer about 20 minutes until soft. The taste can be quite different and often better.

Naked Beans

Legumes are delicious if they are prepared properly and cooked well. Homegrown beans do not need as much soaking or cooking as purchased beans do. Relatively fresh beans absorb all the water they can in four hours.

Overnight soaking is convenient, and probably necessary for store-bought beans, which may have been in storage for years. Soaking water should be three to four times the volume of beans. Wash the beans in a strainer and discard any debris. Place beans in a large pot to soak.

After soaking, drain and rinse the beans. Discard soaking liquid. Cover them with the same amount of fresh cold water. Do not add salt until beans are at the desired doneness. (Many ingredients tend to halt the tenderizing process. Likewise, sauces. It's best to cook the beans, then season them or add them to a sauce.)

Bring the pot to a boil, reduce the heat and keep partially covered to prevent foaming. (Adding 1 Tbsp vegetable oil per cup of beans before cooking will also prevent foaming.) (Soybeans, especially, tend to bubble up through the pressure valve in pressure cooking.)

The texture of cooked beans greatly affects their appeal, so cooking time is important. Depending on the type of bean, how you'll use it and the texture you want, you'll cook beans for different lengths of time. Most homegrown beans do well with about 50 minutes, and rarely need an hour. This leaves a little chewiness to complement their taste. Commercial varieties will likely take closer to 2 hours; chick-peas may take longer; soybeans need about 90 minutes. We've included further guidelines under specific bean types that follow—lentils, favas, etc. A good test for doneness is to let a bean cool, and press it lightly between the tongue and roof of the mouth. If it breaks easily, it's done.

A pressure cooker will reduce cooking time. Make sure the pot is no more than half full. Cook at 15 pounds pressure for 15 to 25 minutes. Pressure-cooked beans will be tender-skinned and soft-textured.

Beans and Vegetables Together

We like sautéing because direct heat brings out the vegetables' oils, especially for potent ones like onions and garlic, yet allows harsher flavours to evaporate. A slow sauté at medium heat will bring veggies to their peak of flavour, which is sealed by a small portion of oil or butter. We generally use unsalted butter, or olive, safflower or canola oil. To reduce fat intake, sauté foods in a liquid (water, stock, low-sodium soy sauce) over medium to medium-high heat. We often begin a sauté, then add a bit of liquid to finish the cooking. In all cases, stir frequently to prevent scorching or sticking and avoid overcooking! Vegetables should be on the crunchy side to retain nutrients and enzymes, which help digestion. It's for this reason that we seldom peel vegetables unless they have been waxed. Most nutrients are stored just beneath the skin.

Prepare vegetables ahead of time. Wash non-organic vegetables with soap and scrub

Sound Nutrition

Because our food is raised without pesticides, we don't have to peel our vegetables before cooking, which saves their nutritional value. If you can't get organic produce, you can use biodegradable detergent or diluted apple cider vinegar and a vegetable brush to wash fruits and vegetables, to reduce the effect of pesticide residues.

Other tips to maximize nutrition: don't discard the seeds; avoid overcooking; eat raw vegetables every day.

in cold water. Don't let vegetables sit in water too long to avoid leaching nutrients. Cut vegetables as desired—slice, chop, dice or grate. Heat the oil or cooking liquid until it steams slightly, then add the food, stirring quickly to coat everything. Add extra liquid in small quantities, no more than $1/4$ cup at a time.

Unless a recipe specifies otherwise, there is an optimum order for adding ingredients. Approximate cooking time is in brackets.

- onions, leeks, scallions and shallots (till translucent)

- ground spices, such as cumin, coriander, curry, etc. (2 min)

- carrots, turnips, beets or other root vegetables (3–5 min)

- celery and brassicas, e.g. cabbage, broccoli, cauliflower (2 min)

- peas, green beans, summer squash, peppers (2 min)

- tomatoes (1 min)

- mushrooms (3 min)

- fresh or dried herbs (1 min)

Garlic is a special consideration and can be added anywhere along the line depending on how strong you desire or can tolerate it. Many of the recipes direct you to sauté garlic at the same time as onions. However, true garlic gourmets add garlic right near the end, just before the herbs, to keep its potency and distinctive flavour.

Scandinavian Beans

SERVES 3–4

This a traditional northern European method of preparing beans that works well for rich and nutty tasting varieties.

---

1 cup brown beans

---

¹/₂ Tbsp butter

---

2 Tbsp brown sugar

---

1 Tbsp cider vinegar

---

salt to taste

---

flour, enough to thicken

❖ After soaking the beans, heat them to boiling and simmer them until tender. Drain and add the remaining ingredients. Serve hot.

Variation: You can substitute the same amount of oil for the butter; molasses or honey for the sugar. Try adding 1–2 cinnamon sticks to the cooking beans for added flavour.

Variation: Create your own sweet bean recipe by adding grated apple and/or carrot, ketchup or tomato sauce, minced garlic and summer savory, to taste.

Grower's Delight

Among the available brown beans we love are Swedish, Dutch, Norwegian and Nez Perce. All these varieties are among the earliest maturing beans Salt Spring Seeds offers.

The now-famous Boston Baked Beans dish was popularized by North America's first European settlers, who adapted a Native bean dish that was baked overnight with deer fat and onions. They used small white haricot, navy or kidney beans, replaced the deer fat with pork and added brown sugar and seasonings.

Honeyed Baked Beans

SERVES 4

Try this recipe with limas. Then experiment with other beans and complementary seasonings.

1 cup dried beans

2 Tbsp oil

1 large onion, sliced

1/2 tsp dry mustard

3 Tbsp honey

salt and pepper to taste

❖ Soak and cook the beans. Drain and reserve the cooking liquid. Preheat oven to 350°F.

Sauté the onion in the oil until just beginning to brown. Stir in the mustard and honey, salt and pepper. Add the beans and enough of their cooking liquid to barely cover.

Transfer to a casserole and bake, covered, 40–50 minutes. Bake uncovered for an additional 10–15 minutes if needed, to reduce liquid.

Variations: Use red kidney beans; omit the mustard and honey; add 1 1/2 Tbsp paprika, 1 bay leaf and 1 more onion (remove bay leaf before serving). Or use pinto beans; omit the mustard and honey; sauté 2 cloves finely chopped garlic with the onions or add the garlic right before baking.

Chili Beans

SERVES 3

Stewing beans on the stove is a fast alternative to baking them. Try Agate Pintos in this recipe—rich and spicy!

1 cup dried pinto beans

3 Tbsp oil

1 onion, chopped

2 cloves garlic, minced

¹/₂ tsp salt

1 tsp chili powder, or to taste

1 tsp ground cumin

1 green pepper, diced

❖ Cook and drain the beans. Sauté the onion and garlic until onion is translucent. Add spices and sauté 2 minutes, then add pepper and sauté 10 minutes. Add beans and sauté slowly another 10 minutes.

Variation: Substitute 1 tsp kelp powder and 1 tsp other powdered seaweed for the chili and cumin.

Food for Thought

"Since World War II, the governing agricultural doctrine in government offices, universities, and corporations has been that 'there are too many people on the farm.' This idea has supported, if indeed it has not caused, one of the most consequential migrations of history: millions of rural people moving from country to city in a stream that has not slackened from the war's end until now. And the strongest force behind this migration then as now, has been economic ruin on the farm . . .

The farm-to-city migration has obviously produced advantages to the corporate economy. The absent farmers have had to be replaced by machinery, petroleum, chemicals, credit, and other expensive goods and services from the agribusiness economy, which ought not to be confused with the economy of what used to be called farming."

— Wendell Berry,
What Are People For?

Refried Beans

SERVES 4–6

This title is a translation of frijoles refritos, but it can be misleading as the beans are fried only once. Refried beans are basic in Mexican cooking and appear in many concoctions, including tacos, and as a side dish with almost everything else.

3–4 Tbsp oil or butter

3 cups cooked pinto, kidney, or pink (such as Santa Maria Pinquito) beans, cooking liquid reserved

❖ In a large iron skillet, heat enough of the oil or butter to cover the bottom. Add 1 cup of cooked beans and, with heat on medium, begin mashing and cooking the beans. As they turn to a paste, continue mashing in more beans, about 1/2 cup at a time. From time to time, work in 1/4 cup of the bean liquid to keep the mixture soft. If the beans start to stick to the bottom, lower the heat slightly and add a little more oil. When all the beans have been mashed in (you can leave a few whole or in pieces for texture), add a little more liquid and turn the heat very low. Allow the mixture to simmer another 15–20 minutes until the bean liquid has been reduced and is part of the bean puree. When a slight crust forms around the edges and on the bottom of the pan, the beans are ready to serve.

Stir in desired seasonings such as salt, pepper, chili powder, relish, chopped onion, etc.

Peas

The most commonly available dried peas are split green or yellow, the latter being a little milder in flavour. Some commercial outlets also offer whole dried peas. For growers, there are many whole pea varieties available that are excellent for soup. Whole peas can be substituted for split peas in any recipe, and can replace beans in most.

Grower's Delight

Golden Sweet Edible Pod Pea has a unique yellow pod that, when young, makes a colourful and delectable addition to stir-frys. The mature pea is an especially good soup pea.

Pea Soup

SERVES 4

1 onion, sliced

1 clove garlic, minced

1 bay leaf

1 Tbsp oil

1 cup dried peas

4 cups water

1 celery stalk, sliced

1 carrot, sliced thin

$^1/_2$ tsp thyme, dill or sage

salt and pepper to taste

❖ In a soup pot, sauté onion, garlic and bay leaf in oil for 5 minutes. Add remaining ingredients and simmer for 1 hour, stirring occasionally to prevent sticking.

Soybeans

Soybeans can be substituted for other dried beans in many of our recipes. They are more filling than pintos or kidneys because they are higher in both protein and oil. For this reason, when substituting soybeans for other legumes you can reduce the required amount by a third.

We've found that black soybeans are enhanced by garlic, ginger and cumin, whereas other soybeans are complemented by tomato, basil and oregano.

Homegrown soybeans need about 90 minutes' simmering after an overnight soaking to be cooked *al dente*. You'll have to experiment with commercial types, but most need about 3 hours' cooking.

Baked Soybeans

SERVES 4

1 cup dried soybeans, soaked

2 Tbsp butter

1 onion, chopped

*1 medium tomato, chopped,
or $^1/_4$ cup tomato paste or ketchup*

$^1/_4$ cup molasses

1 Tbsp soy sauce

1 tsp dry mustard

$^1/_2$ tsp salt

$^1/_4$ tsp black pepper

❖ Cook the soybeans and drain, reserving $^1/_4$ cup cooking liquid. Preheat oven to 350°F.

Combine beans, liquid and remaining ingredients in a casserole dish and bake, covered, for 30 minutes, then uncovered for 45 minutes.

Variation: Try adding any or all of the following: a couple of finely chopped cloves garlic; a chopped green or red sweet pepper; $^1/_2$ cup corn kernels.

Lentils

Lentils are a popular source of protein in many world cuisines. In the Middle East they are most often used in soups and stews, frequently flavoured with lemon, olive oil and garlic. In south India, lentils are used for breads, fritters, salads, pancakes and vegetable dishes.

Lentils need no soaking and cook relatively quickly—from 20 minutes to an hour, depending on the variety. Try simmering them with a bay leaf. Watch them carefully because they soften easily (fine for soups, but not for main dishes). When they are cooked, add a little butter and lemon juice. Season with Spike, paprika, pepper, soy sauce, etc. and remove the bay leaf.

Simple Lentil Soup

SERVES 6

1 cup dried lentils

2 onions, chopped

2 cloves garlic, chopped

1 bay leaf

2 quarts water

¹/₂ tsp fresh lemon juice

❖ Combine all ingredients in a medium saucepan and simmer gently for 1 hour, or until the lentils are tender.

Favas

Favas are sometimes confused with lima beans, though taste-wise they're more a cross between peas and limas. As with many legumes that can be eaten fresh or dry, some varieties are better in one state than the other. Windsor, the most commonly available commercial variety, is passable in its fresh green state but is thick-skinned and mealy when cooked as a dry bean.

Don't use favas fresh if they've formed a yellowish-green skin. Use them as dry beans. Also, some varieties have a light green outer part that should be removed before eating the dark green part inside.

Store-bought favas need a long soaking and many hours' cooking, but homegrown ones require only 60 to 90 minutes' simmering after an overnight soak. One thing about favas is that overcooking will not make them mushy. The seedcoat retains a chewiness that can range from pleasantly chewy to unpleasantly tough, depending on the variety.

As for taste, the best varieties are rich, earthy and sweet, and easily the equal of any other bean.

Note

The skin of our favourite dried favas admirably complements the inner texture, but you may find varieties where this is not true. To remove the skins, boil the favas for 2 minutes and let them sit in the hot water for 30–45 minutes. Cool in water and peel. (A tip from the Aprovecho Institute, a group in Oregon especially knowledgeable about fava beans.)

Note

Very few people are allergic to beans, but there is a possibility of allergic reaction to virtually any food you introduce to your diet. New or unusual body reactions or emotional swings any time up to twenty-four hours after eating the food may indicate an allergic response. A response may need immediate attention, or be so mild it is simply worth noting for comparison next time you eat the food.

Fava beans were grown by the ancient Egyptians and Chinese, as well as by the Greeks and Romans. Today, favas are a popular crop in India, Burma, Mexico and Brazil. Millions of people in the Middle East eat them daily, where they're traditionally prepared with lemon, olive oil and garlic. Since 1990, we've tested many different dry favas, so we know that people all over the world eat them because they taste so good!

Ful Medames

SERVES 3–4

This basic fava bean salad uses ingredients typical of Middle Eastern fava dishes and is traditionally served with hard-boiled eggs and parsley.

$^1/_2$ cup dried fava beans, soaked

4 Tbsp olive or flax oil

juice of $^1/_2$ lemon

2 cloves garlic, crushed or finely chopped

❖ Cook beans until soft (about $1^1/_2$ hours if homegrown; $2^1/_2$–3 hours if store-bought). Drain well. Dress with oil, lemon and garlic. Let cool.

Variation: Substitute chick-peas or Black Turtle beans for favas; use half the oil; substitute dill for garlic. Try adding a chopped small onion, a pinch of cayenne pepper and chopped parsley.

Chick-peas

Chick-peas, or garbanzo beans, come in different colours. The common light beige variety has a rich, full flavour that makes it perfect for pâtés, casseroles and soups. The black and green ones we've tried are less satisfying.

Commercial chick-peas need about 2½ hours' cooking after an overnight soaking. For homegrown varieties, 90 minutes is generally sufficient.

Chick-pea Simplicity

SERVES 4–5

1 Tbsp olive oil

1 onion, chopped

1 large leek, chopped

2 tomatoes, chopped

1 cup dried chick-peas, soaked

3 cups water or stock

❖ Heat the oil and sauté the onion, leek and tomatoes until very soft. Add the chick-peas and stock. Bring to the boil and simmer until the chick-peas are soft—1½ to 3 hours, depending on variety.

Sieve or purée the soup in a processor, then return to the pot and reheat.

Grains

North American wheats and barleys are generally harvested, hulled and processed into flour to make other products. However, there are grain varieties that can be hulled easily by hand. Eaten whole, these foods retain their full nutritional value and fibre content.

Both wheat and barley make a good addition to cooked rice in the proportion of 1 to 3. Because of their chewiness, they may take some getting used to for those only accustomed to soft grains like millet or rice. It is this very chewiness, though, that we like the best about them.

Unlike our beans, the barleys we grow take longer to cook and are chewier than standard commercial varieties. Grocery stores rarely carry anything but products from wheat flour and processed pearl or pot barley. For more substantial wheatberries and barleys, check local health food stores and natural, organic markets.

Our other favourite grains are amaranth and quinoa, which are to grains what soybeans are to legumes. They've been used in Central and Southern American cultures for over 5,000 years but are relative newcomers to the North American scene. People are growing these grains all over the continent now. Our local supermarket carries amaranth in bulk, and several companies now offer packaged quinoa through health food and natural food outlets.

Wheat

Despite the millions of agricultural acres allotted to wheat in North America, very few people cook whole wheat "berries," or seeds, which have the full nutritional value intact.

Cooked wheatberries make a very satisfying meal with just a little butter, soy sauce or other seasoning. They also make good sprouts.

Basic Stove-Top Wheat

SERVES 4–6

Whole wheat will not soften up to the extent that barley does after longer cooking. Its texture is pleasant and gives the mouth a nice little workout. Always add salt after cooking wheat or it will not absorb the cooking water. For the same reason, cook with water, not broth.

2¹/₂ cups water

---

1 cup wheat

---

¹/₂ tsp salt (optional)

❖ In a 2-quart saucepan, bring water to boil. Stir in wheat, return to boiling, then simmer for 90 minutes or until all liquid has been absorbed. Remove from heat and let stand, covered, 10 minutes. Add salt if desired, and fluff with a fork.

Barley

Barley is usually found in recipes titled "hearty." Its pleasant earthy flavour, its toothiness and the satisfaction it gives makes it a good candidate for a substantial meal. It is higher in protein, vitamins and fibre than rice, corn or wheat and is every bit as versatile as rice.

Hulless barley, the kind we call for in the recipes, can be difficult to find in stores but is the most nutritious and satisfying to our palate. Of the pot and pearl barley you are likely to find, pot barley is the least processed, and is darker in colour than the pearled variety. The texture of cooked barley will vary according to variety as well as the amount of water used in cooking—from a soft, starchy porridge to chewy separate grains.

Barley's musky flavour is enhanced by parsley, chives, bay leaves and basil, but it combines well with bold seasonings such as fennel, garlic, anise, caraway, cloves, rosemary and thyme. Its thickening properties enrich soups and stews and make it appropriate for molded salads. Because of its assertive taste, it is best used as a side dish to meat, fish or dairy foods, not mixed with them.

Basic Stove-Top Barley

SERVES 4–6

This will make about 4 cups whole barley. Using store-bought pearl barley in the same recipe will yield about 3¹/₄ cups. Pre-soaking barley shortens the cooking time.

2¹/₂ cups water

1 cup hulless barley

1 tsp salt (optional)

❖ In a 2-quart saucepan, bring the water and salt to a boil. Stir in barley and return to boiling. Reduce heat, cover and simmer for 1 hour or until almost all of the liquid has been absorbed. Remove from heat and let stand, covered, for 10 minutes. Add salt if desired, and fluff with a fork.

Food for Thought

"While many may ponder the consequences of global warming, perhaps the biggest single environmental catastrophe in human history is unfolding in the garden . . . Loss of genetic diversity in agriculture— silent, rapid, inexorable— is leading us to a rendezvous with extinction—to the doorstep of hunger on a scale we refuse to imagine. To simplify the environment as we have done with agriculture is to destroy the complex interrelationships that hold the natural world together. Reducing the diversity of life, we narrow our options for the future and render our own survival more precarious."

— Cary Fowler and Pat Mooney, *Shattering*

Lentil Soup with Barley

SERVES 3–4

3 cloves garlic, finely chopped

1 large onion, chopped

1 celery stalk, chopped

*1/4 cup celery leaves
or 1 Tbsp lovage leaves, chopped*

2 carrots, sliced thick

3 Tbsp oil or butter

1 1/2 cups dried lentils

1/3 cup barley

3 Tbsp brewer's yeast

2 Tbsp chopped fresh parsley

5 whole cloves (optional)

❖ Sauté vegetables in oil or butter until fragrant. Add lentils, barley, yeast, parsley, cloves and enough water to cover by 3 inches. Simmer covered for 45–60 minutes.

Variation: For a more fragrant, robust soup, try adding shredded green leafy vegetables such as collards, kale, spinach or beet greens; and 1–2 Tbsp miso just before serving.

Quinoa

Quinoa is a disk-shaped seed with bands around the periphery. It is easy to digest, has a wonderful flavour, and cooks up whole, like rice, in 15 minutes. When cooked, the bands partially separate but retain their curved shape, which "covers" the grain with spiral and crescent moon shapes. This "coat" offers just enough tooth resistance to make quinoa's texture similar to wild rice. This coat is also covered with a bitter substance called "saponin" which calls for rinsing. Most commercial varieties are ready to cook.

Cooked quinoa expands almost five times its dry volume and turns transparent. Before cooking, prepare the grain as follows:

Commercial quinoa: Place grain in large pot. Run warm water into pot to agitate grain without spilling. Drain well.

Homegrown quinoa: Place grain in blender with some water. Blend at low speed. Add water. Blend again. Add water. Repeat 3 or 4 times and drain well.

Basic Quinoa

SERVES 3–4

1 cup quinoa

1 cup water

❖ Rinse quinoa as directed above. Place rinsed quinoa and water in a saucepan and bring to a boil. Cover and simmer 10–12

Sound Nutrition

Quinoa contains 16 percent protein, E and B vitamins, calcium, iron and phosphorus.

*Try using cooked ama-
ranth or toasted quinoa as a
substitute for nuts in about
equal quantity. This is a
great way to reduce fats
and increase nutrition in
baked goods! And a satisfying substitute for the many
people who are allergic to
nuts.*

minutes till all water is absorbed. A little more water will give a softer texture.

Grain Hash with Squash

❖ Cook quinoa until the liquid is almost gone. Add an equal volume of cooked squash. Add sautéed onion to taste, stir and serve.

Grain à la Grecque

SERVES 4

❖ To cooked quinoa, add equal amounts by volume: pitted olives, diced Spanish onion/chopped leeks/onion greens, crumbled feta cheese, finely chopped red pepper. Add oregano to taste and mix thoroughly. Add oil and vinegar dressing if desired, and serve.

Toasted Quinoa

❖ Place rinsed quinoa into a large skillet and cook over medium heat, shaking occasionally, for 15 minutes or until golden brown. Cool completely. Use like other nuts and seeds.

Amaranth

Amaranth is a first-rate source of both grain and leaf protein. Its seed contains over 15 percent protein—more than any other grain except quinoa. The grain cooks up simply like quinoa, can be prepared in similar ways and is even more delicious. It is not covered by saponin so does not require any lengthy rinsing procedure.

Amaranth flour contains more gluten than quinoa flour and combines well with traditional flours in the ratio of 1 to 4. Toasted and milled amaranth makes a hearty cooked cereal.

Basic Amaranth

SERVES 3–4

1 cup amaranth

1 cup water

❖ Add amaranth to gently boiling water, cover and simmer gently for 10 minutes. For a more porridge-like consistency, use a greater proportion of water. Experiment to find the texture you prefer.

Variations: Try adding cooked amaranth to rice for a pleasing, crunchy texture. Or mix it with briefly sautéed carrots, scallions or celery, with a bit of oil or butter. Or add it to mashed potatoes (about 1/2 cup amaranth per 3 medium potatoes), with sautéed onion if desired.

You can substitute amaranth for quinoa

Food for Thought

"It is reasonable to ask how much has been accomplished in the introduction or creation of new economic species in the last five thousand years, that is, since 3000 BC. In spite of recent [agricultural] advances . . . and notwithstanding the admittedly greater intelligence through which our crops have been made more adaptable to the demands of modern agriculture, it has to be admitted that not a single species comparable to bread wheat, Indian corn, rice or the soybean, or in fact to any of our important food annuals has been added by modern man to the economic flora of the world."

— Edgar Anderson,
Plants, Man and Life

If you grow your own grains, you'll want to try amaranth greens. Quinoa greens make a tasty salad high in vitamins and minerals. Amaranth leaves are even more nutritious, higher in calcium and iron than just about any vegetable.

in Grain Hash (see page 55), but add toasted chopped almonds instead of onion. And try Grain à la Grecque (page 55) with amaranth instead of quinoa.

Steamed Amaranth Greens

SERVES 4

6 cups amaranth greens

1 onion, chopped

2 cloves garlic, finely chopped

1 Tbsp oil

❖ Coarsely chop amaranth. Sauté garlic and onion in oil over medium high heat. Add amaranth, stir thoroughly, and reduce heat. Cover and steam the greens about 5 minutes.

Garlic

Garlic is a staple seasoning in cuisines around the world. In cooking, it is unique in that it can be added anywhere along the line according to taste. Many people sauté garlic at the same time as onions. However, since it keeps its potency and distinctiveness best when added at the end of cooking, we usually add it just before the fresh herbs. It's simply a matter of taste. It may also have to do with what you're doing afterwards, or whether you're a nursing mother!

Regarding garlic, a Mrs. W. G. Waters commented in *The Cook's Decameron* (1920): "Garlic used as it should be used is the soul, the divine essence, of cookery. The cook who can employ it succesfully will be found to possess the delicacy of perception, the accuracy of judgment, and the dexterity of hand which go to the formation of a great artist."

Grower's Delight

You can use 1–2 Tbsp minced garlic greens in place of a clove of garlic. If you grow garlic, cutting the flower heads that emerge allows the plant to put more energy into forming the bulb. These greens can be used as chives or onion, a special treat during June and July. Watch for them in supermarkets too. They're a special addition to a stir-fry!

Garlic Yogurt Sauce

This quick sauce is open to many herb additions. It's great for dipping veggie sticks and makes a good accompaniment to most vegetable, fish and meat dishes.

2–3 cloves garlic

salt and pepper to taste

1 cup plain yogurt

¹/₂ cup sour cream

¹/₂ cup chopped mixed fresh herbs—chervil, dill, tarragon, etc.

❖ Pound the garlic with a mortar and pestle, or mince and then mash well with the flat of a cleaver. Place the mashed garlic in a bowl, season lightly, then stir in yogurt, sour cream and mixed herbs, blending well.

Cover and let stand at room temperature or refrigerate for at least 2 hours.

Garlic Butter

MAKES ⅓ CUP

⅓ cup butter, softened slightly

1 Tbsp minced garlic

2 drops each Worcestershire and hot pepper sauce

¼ tsp Dijon mustard

❖ Mash together all ingredients in a small bowl. Taste and add more seasonings for spicier butter.

The Recipes

Bread and Breakfast

We hope this section helps you let go of any idea that breakfast has to come from a box or the freezer. Though many of us eat on the run, or just plain skip breakfast, there are days when an energizing, nutritious meal is called for. Children, especially, need a healthy start to the day.

One of the drawbacks of using wheat or barley as a cereal is the cooking time. Amaranth and quinoa cook a bit faster. But even better, prepare an extra portion of beans or grain while cooking dinner—it may be just the headstart you need when mornings are tightly scheduled or rushed.

Because of their high protein content, the breads in this section are handy to have on hand for a quick meal. Bake them up in advance and freeze in meal-size portions for an excellent nutritional start to the day.

Bean Bread

MAKES 1 LOAF

1 1/2 cups cooked beans

1/2 cup butter

1/4 cup honey

1 egg

1/2 tsp salt

1 3/4 cups whole wheat flour

2 tsp baking powder

1/2 tsp cinnamon

1/2 tsp nutmeg

1/4 tsp ground ginger

❖ Preheat oven to 350°F. Mash the beans with enough water or stock to make them moist but not soupy. Cream the butter and honey. Beat in egg. Add dry ingredients and beat on high speed with an electric mixer for 4 minutes. Spread into a greased and floured loaf pan and bake 45 minutes.

Pan Bread

MAKES 1 ROUND LOAF

¹/₂ cup dried beans

6 Tbsp oil

1 large onion, chopped

2 cloves garlic, minced

1 egg, beaten

1 cup corn meal

2 tsp baking powder

1 Tbsp chili powder

¹/₂ tsp ground cumin

¹/₂ tsp salt

¹/₃ cup grated cheese

¹/₄ cup sliced olives

❖ Cook beans and drain them, reserving ³/₄ cup liquid. Preheat oven to 350°F. Heat 2 Tbsp of the oil in an oven-proof skillet and sauté the onion and garlic until the onion is translucent. Remove half the onion and garlic to a bowl and add cooked beans, the reserved liquid, egg, the remaining 4 Tbsp oil, corn meal, baking powder, chili powder, cumin and salt. Mix well, return to the skillet and bake about 15 minutes. Just before done, sprinkle with grated cheese and olives. Continue baking until the cheese melts.

Soy Milk

We've tested many soybeans over the years to find a superior brand for making soy milk. We've discovered that what may be barely passable as an eating bean can be excellent for milk. The best we've found to date is milk from black soybeans. It's a rich, mocha-tasting grey-brown milk that can stand on its own without honey or vanilla. If you can't find black soybeans, do up small batches of different varieties to find one you like.

---

³/4 cup soybeans

---

4 cups water, or less for a richer milk

---

¹/4 cup honey, or to taste

---

1 tsp vanilla

❖ Soak soybeans overnight. Drain.

Liquefy half the beans with 2 cups of the water in blender, then strain through 2 layers of cheesecloth to extract all liquid. Repeat process with the rest of the beans and the remaining 2 cups water. (Save the "pulp," known as "okara," for making soups.)

Add honey and vanilla to the soy milk and simmer, covered, 30 minutes. Refrigerate.

Note: Soy milk will keep up to a week refrigerated, but for best flavour use the milk within a day or two.

Note

If you aren't up to making your own soy milk, there are several soy and rice milks or beverages available in health and natural food outlets. Try them as a substitutes in baking. You'll never know the difference!

Lemony Date Wheatberry Cereal

SERVES 3–4

This cereal enlivens the taste buds as well as the body for a good start to the day!

1 cup wheatberries (or 3 cups cooked)

2 cups water

1 cup chopped dates

1 tsp grated lemon rind

juice of 1 lemon, or to taste

1 Tbsp maple syrup, or to taste

❖ Cook wheatberries in 2 cups water for about 1 hour, or heat the 3 cups cooked wheatberries. Add the remaining ingredients, stir and serve.

Amaranth Coconut Pineapple Loaf

MAKES 1 LOAF

This loaf is moist and nutritious. Because it's not too sweet, it can be a healthy snack, a quick breakfast—with cream cheese perhaps—or a light dessert.

1 cup all-purpose flour

1 cup amaranth flour

2 tsp baking powder

1 tsp salt

¹/₂ cooked amaranth

²/₃ cup honey

1 egg

²/₃ cup milk or soy milk

¹/₃ cup vegetable oil

1 tsp vanilla extract

¹/₂ cup shredded coconut

¹/₂ cup pineapple tidbits

❖ Preheat oven to 350°F. In a large bowl, combine the flours, baking powder and salt. Add the amaranth and drizzle honey over both, working them into the flour with a wooden spoon. In a medium bowl beat the egg, milk, oil and vanilla. Turn the wet into the dry ingredients and stir until well com-

"Eaters . . . must understand that eating takes place inescapably in the world, that it is inescapably an agricultural act, and that how we eat determines, to a considerable extent, how the world is used."

— Wendell Berry,
What Are People For?

bined. Stir in the coconut and pineapple, mix well and spread in a greased or treated loaf pan. Bake 45–50 minutes, or until a toothpick inserted in the centre comes out clean. Turn onto a rack to cool.

Amaranth Pancakes

MAKES ABOUT 8 – 4″ PANCAKES

¹/₂ cup all-purpose flour

¹/₂ cup amaranth flour

1¹/₂ tsp baking soda

¹/₂ tsp salt

1 egg

³/₄ cup milk or soy milk

2 Tbsp oil

2 Tbsp honey

❖ Combine the flours, baking soda and salt in a large bowl.

In a separate, smaller bowl, beat the egg, adding milk, oil and honey.

Add milk mixture to flour mixture and stir till just blended. Grease a large skillet and heat to medium-high. Drop batter by large spoonfuls into skillet and cook till bubbles form. Turn and cook lightly on the other side.

Barley Pudding

SERVES 6

$1^1/_3$ cups milk

$^1/_8$ tsp salt

$^1/_4$ cup brown sugar

1 Tbsp butter

1 tsp vanilla

2 eggs, lightly beaten

2 cups cooked barley, cooled

$^1/_3$ cup raisins

$^1/_2$ tsp grated lemon rind

1 tsp lemon juice

❖ Preheat oven to 325°F. Combine the milk, salt, sugar, butter, vanilla and eggs, beating well. Add the barley, raisins, lemon rind and lemon juice. Turn into a well-greased loaf pan. Set the pan in a larger baking pan in the oven. Pour hot water into the large pan to within $^3/_4$ inch of the top of the custard. Bake until a knife inserted in the centre comes out clean (about 1 hour). Serve hot or cold.

"The promise of the Green Revolution has since faded to a toxic brownout. Four decades of a chemical-dependent hayride have devastated the country's soil. Far worse than the infamous Dust Bowl of the 1930s, U.S. topsoil is being depleted at the terrifying rate of an inch a year, an annual loss of an area the size of Connecticut. Millions of years in the making, an estimated 75 percent of topsoil has vanished since the Europeans set foot, livestock, and plough on the continent. Meanwhile, a third of cropland is exhibiting marked decline in productivity. Historically, topsoil depletion has been a root cause in a demise of several civilizations."

— Kenny Ausubel,
Seeds of Change

Quinoa Pudding

SERVES 4–6

3 cups cooked quinoa

1 cup milk

¹/₃ cup honey

3 eggs, beaten

1 Tbsp butter

1 tsp vanilla

¹/₂ cup raisins

1 tsp cinnamon

pinch of nutmeg and cloves

❖ Preheat oven to 350°F. Combine all ingredients. Pour into greased 1-quart baking dish. Bake until set, about 45 minutes. Serve with milk or yogurt, if desired.

Variation: Substitute amaranth for the quinoa.

Nutri-Blueberry Muffins

MAKES 12 MUFFINS

The quinoa gives these muffins a pleasantly chewy texture. They're moist and not too sweet.

1 cup quinoa

1 cup corn meal

1^1/$_4$ cups boiling water

^{3}/$_4$ cup amaranth flour

^{1}/$_2$ cup all-purpose flour

2 tsp baking soda

^{1}/$_2$ tsp salt

1 large egg, beaten

^{1}/$_4$ cup vegetable oil

^{1}/$_4$ cup honey

grated rind of 1 orange

^{1}/$_2$ cup blueberries

❖ Rinse the quinoa till little foam remains. In a medium bowl, combine the quinoa and cornmeal with the water. Stir to moisten and let stand, covered, for 1 hour.

Preheat oven to 350°F. In a large bowl, combine the flours, baking soda and salt. In a small bowl, beat the egg, then beat in the oil, honey and orange rind. Stir the egg mixture into the quinoa. Pour into the flour

Quinoa contains 16 percent protein, E and B vitamins, calcium, iron and phosphorus.

mixture, beating only till mixed. Fold in the blueberries. Spoon into greased or treated muffin tins and bake 30 minutes, or till golden and a toothpick comes out clean.

Quinoa Cereal

SERVES 3–4

2 cups cooked quinoa

1 apple, seeded and chopped

¹/₂ cup raisins

¹/₂ tsp cinnamon

❖ Combine all ingredients and serve with milk or yogurt if desired.

Healthy Snacks and Appetizers

Snacks in this culture are perhaps among the most hazardous of foods given our passion for either high-fat and -sodium or sweet packaged products. Having a few things on hand that can qualify as veggie dips or sandwich fillings can add valuable nutrients to your diet and, when prepared along with a regular meal, are convenient and time-saving.

Our favourite snacks tend to be high-fibre fresh fruit or simple, unadorned veggies. Pesto, aioli or humous can turn a simple vegetable, cracker or piece of bread into a highly nutritious gourmet treat. (Or try thin slices of homegrown garlic on toast, with or without cheese—mmm!) Likewise, a bean spread or pâté is not only a great way to use leftover beans, but an economical and satisfying sandwich filling for lunch.

For occasions when you'd like to serve something "special," baked garlic on toast rounds or quinoa fritters are the ticket. These scrumptious tidbits are interesting and innovative preludes to any meal.

Soynuts

SERVES 4

1/2 cup dried soybeans, soaked, cooked just until tender, and drained

1/2 cup butter

1 clove garlic, minced

1 tsp salt

1 Tbsp soy sauce

❖ Preheat oven to 350°F. Spread soybeans on shallow cookie pan and roast 30 minutes or until browned, stirring occasionally.

Meanwhile, over medium heat, melt butter and cook garlic with salt and soy sauce for 3–4 minutes. Remove from heat and set aside. Drizzle the butter mixture over the beans in a heatproof bowl. Toss gently to coat. Serve at room temperature.

Soynuts can also be made by skipping the last four ingredients and the last paragraph!

Lentil Pâté

SERVES 12–15

1 cup lentils, cooked and drained,
¹/₃ cup liquid reserved

2 Tbsp oil

2 cups finely chopped onion

2 cloves garlic, crushed or finely chopped

¹/₂ cup finely chopped carrots

1 Tbsp water

2 medium tomatoes, finely chopped

¹/₂ cup bread crumbs

¹/₂ tsp salt

¹/₂ tsp ground cumin

pepper to taste

❖ While lentils cook, heat oil in a large skillet over medium heat. Sauté onions and garlic 3–4 minutes, then add carrots and water. Cover and steam until tender. Remove from heat. In a large mixing bowl, combine tomatoes, bread crumbs, lentils, salt, cumin and pepper. Stir in the onions, garlic and carrots. Mix well. Place half the mixture in a food processor and purée with half the reserved liquid. Stir between pulses to break down the lentils. Place the mixture in a pâté dish or half-quart casserole. Repeat process for the rest of the mixture and add to serving dish.

Serve on crackers or as a sandwich filling.

"During the next decade, the core group of snackers—the 10 to 20-year-olds—is projected to grow twice as fast as the overall population. We are introducing products and package sizes especially for this new generation of snackers . . . The overall cost per pound of materials used to produce our products has not increased in the last 10 years."
— 1991 Annual Report, PepsiCo

"PepsiCo is the world's largest supplier of snack food, geared largely to a child market and supported by government-subsidized meal programs in schools. Children, many with unmet needs, pay up to a 5900 percent markup for their products, despite the fact that their materials costs have not increased. PepsiCo sells soft drinks and operates 29,000 fast-food restaurants around the globe. Their CEO claims they have doubled their sales and net income every 5 years for 26 years. The company intends to double their growth every 5 years 'forever'."
—John Robbins, *Diet for a New World*

Fava Spread

SERVES 8–12

4 cups cooked favas

2 large tomatoes, chopped

2 sweet onions, chopped

1/2 cup feta cheese

1 tsp ground cumin

juice of 2 lemons

1/4 cup oil

seasonings to taste

❖ Combine beans with the other ingredients and mash thoroughly. Spread it on crackers or stuff pita breads.

Humous

SERVES 6–8

Humous or pureed chick-peas is a Middle Eastern dish that has many variations. It's usually served on Arab or pita bread but is good as a spread on other breads and crackers or as a dip for raw vegetables. This recipe is one of the most basic.

2 cups cooked chick-peas

1 clove garlic

¼ cup lemon juice

¼ cup olive oil

2 Tbsp chopped fresh parsley

❖ Purée the chick-peas and garlic in a blender or food processor. Mix in the lemon juice and olive oil. Add a little water if needed to make a soft mixture. Sprinkle the parsley on top and chill at least 1 hour before serving.

Food for Thought

"Adaptability to change is the key to survival, and change is the only constant in nature. Now that human tampering with nature has radically altered the balance of the world, change is occurring at a heightened pace. If, for example, human-induced expansion of deserts doubles by the year 2000, as it has done for the past ten years, then those plants that tolerate heat and drought will assume special new importance.

Variety is not only the spice of life, but the very staff of life. Diversity is nature's fail-safe mechanism against extinction. It provides the vast genetic pool of accumulated experiences and characteristics from which change can originate. Any banker recommends a diversified portfolio in case one stock fails. The most unpredicatable future in history may be upon us, and by diminishing diversity, we are shrinking the genetic pool that is the very source of our biological options for survival."

— Kenny Ausubel,
Seeds of Change

Loving Kindness Humous

SERVES 4

This recipe appears in Dan's book Greening the Garden. *The carrot is the special ingredient.*

1 cup dried chick-peas

1 large carrot, coarsely chopped

3 or more whole cloves garlic

1 bay leaf

juice of 2 lemons

¹/₂ cup sesame tahini

5 or more cloves garlic, crushed or finely chopped

salt to taste

❖ Soak chick-peas in 3 cups cold water for at least 4 hours. Rinse and add fresh water to cover. Boil for 1¹/₂ hours with coarsely chopped carrot, whole garlic cloves and bay leaf, until very tender. Drain, reserving cooking liquid.

Remove bay leaf and mash chick-peas, carrot and garlic while still hot. Stir in the lemon juice, tahini and crushed garlic. Add small amounts of cooking liquid until humous reaches desired consistency. Salt to taste. Cool in refrigerator.

Serve with whole grain crackers or Arab (pita) bread as an appetizer or snack. Makes good lunch sandwiches too.

Quinoa Fritters

SERVES 4–5

2 cups cooked quinoa, cooled

1/2 cup freshly grated Parmesan cheese

2 Tbsp finely chopped shallots, leeks or onions

1/4 cup finely chopped fresh parsley

1 Tbsp poppy seeds

salt, pepper, seasoning to taste

sesame seeds

3/4 cup oil

salsa

❖ Combine all ingredients except oil, sesame seeds and salsa. Shape mixture into small firm patties. Coat both sides lightly with sesame seeds.

Heat oil in a skillet over medium-high heat until hot but not smoking. Fry patties, turning as seeds colour. Remove and drain on paper towels. Serve hot with salsa.

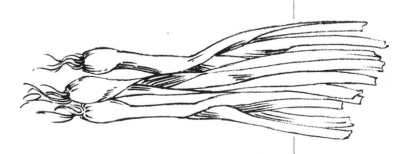

Garlic Cheese Spread

MAKES 1¹/₂ CUPS

1 cup cream cheese, softened

¹/₂ cup sour cream

3 cloves garlic, crushed

2 Tbsp minced fresh parsley

salt and pepper to taste

❖ Combine the cream cheese with the sour cream in a small bowl. Add the garlic and parsley, blending well. Add salt and pepper to taste. Cover tightly and refrigerate before serving. Eat it on bread or crackers, or serve it as a dip. Keeps refrigerated (tightly covered) for up to 5 days.

Variation: Adding 1 Tbsp minced basil, dill or tarragon, or 1 tsp herb vinegar, makes for a tangier flavour. Feta or goat cheese can be substituted for half the cream cheese.

Aioli

MAKES 2 CUPS

This famous garlic mayonnaise is ideal as a dip for raw vegetables or as a sauce for fish or steamed vegetables.

¹/₂ cup fresh lemon juice

¹/₂ tsp salt

2 tsp Dijon mustard

4–6 cloves garlic, crushed

2 eggs

1¹/₂ cups olive oil

❖ Blend all ingredients except oil in blender until thoroughly mixed. With blender running, slowly drizzle in oil in a steady flow until it is all incorporated and mixture is thick.

Food for Thought

"*I am making a plea for diversity not only because diversity exists and is pleasant, but also because it is necessary and we need more of it. This is the need of every American rural landscape that I am acquainted with. We need a greater range of species and varieties of plants and animals, of human skills and methods, so that the use may be fitted ever more sensitively and elegantly to the place. Our places, in short, are asking us questions, some of them urgent questions, and we do not have the answers.*"

— Wendell Berry, *What Are People For?*

*You just can't beat the fla-
vour of fresh-grown garlic!
Most of the garlic sold commercially on this continent
is transported up to thousands of miles from Mexico
and California. Yet it's one
of the most carefree crops
you can grow. Garlic does
best planted in the fall for a
midsummer harvest. We
even know of people who've
grown it successfully in containers. A thought for you
apartment dwellers!*

Baked Garlic

SERVES 4

*The slow baking in this recipe gives the garlic a
mild, fragrant and nutty sweet flavour. It can be
used to enhance grilled foods, pizzas, focaccias and
pastas.*

6 garlic bulbs

1/4 cup butter

1/4 cup olive oil

1/2 tsp minced fresh thyme

fresh parsley and thyme sprigs for garnish

❖ Preheat oven to 300°F. Remove the
papery outer skin of garlic but leave the
cloves intact around their central stalk.
Place the bulbs in a small baking dish that
will just contain them. Melt the butter with
the olive oil and thyme. Brush the garlic
bulbs generously with the mixture. Cover
and bake, basting occasionally, until the
cloves are tender, about 1 hour. Uncover
and bake 20 minutes longer. Remove the
garlic heads from the baking dish and whisk
a little water into the baking juices to make
a light sauce. Pour the sauce over the baked
garlic, garnish with sprigs of parsley and
thyme, if desired, and serve.

The softened parts of each clove can be
squeezed from the skin onto buttered bread
and the bread can be dipped into the sauce.
Then spread goat cream cheese on the
bread for a really gourmet treat.

Pesto

MAKES 1¹/₂ CUPS

6 cloves garlic, sliced thin

¹/₃ cup pine nuts

2 cups packed fresh basil leaves

³/₄ cup freshly grated Parmesan cheese

¹/₂ cup olive oil

❖ Place all the ingredients in a food processor or blender and pulse the motor to make a homogeneous sauce which is not as fine as a purée.

If using a mortar and pestle, pound the garlic first, then the pine nuts. Chop the basil and add it by the handful, pounding it in well. Stir in the cheese and oil alternately, a little at a time.

Makes enough for about 8 servings of pasta.

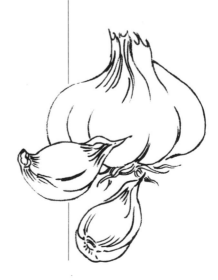

The Recipes

Sumptuous Salads

The word "salad" derives from the Latin "to bring health." We rarely miss a generous raw salad in our daily diet. Nothing is so rich in enzymes. Nor so pleasurable when we can pick fresh greens from the garden just as the rest of our meal is ready—right into the bowl!

The salads here range from light but nutritious combinations of vegetables and grains to substantially filling bean salads. Any one of them, served with a green salad or veggie sticks and a good loaf of bread, makes a wonderful summer dinner or winter lunch.

Cooking time is particularly important for bean salads or you can end up with undifferentiated mush. See "The Basics" for optimum times. Different bean varieties should be cooked separately and mixed afterwards.

Salads that contain different coloured beans are as good to look at as they are to eat!

We hope these recipes inspire your own creations, as both beans and grains combine with so many things. Have fun!

Ful Medames For Six

SERVES 6

3 cups cooked favas

1 cup water

2 cloves garlic, minced

1/4 cup fresh lemon juice

1 tsp ground cumin

cayenne pepper to taste

olive oil

*chopped tomato, scallions, fresh parsley
for garnish*

Dressing:

1/2 cup sesame tahini

1/4 cup water

2 Tbsp fresh lemon juice

1 clove garlic, minced

❖ Combine beans and water. Mix in garlic, lemon juice and cumin. Simmer 25–45 minutes or until beans are soft and creamy. Combine dressing ingredients. Place beans in individual serving bowls. Stir in dressing to taste. Sprinkle with cayenne pepper. Pour olive oil over beans to cover. Serve chopped tomato, scallions and fresh parsley for individual garnishing.

Grower's Delight

Some beans keep their dark colour after cooking, a quality we appreciate, especially for salads. Some two-tone beans, including Aunt Jean's and Wild Goose, retain this pleasing visual contrast after cooking.

Red Bean Reward

SERVES 4

1 cup dried red beans

2 Tbsp olive oil

1 Tbsp red wine vinegar

1 tsp chopped fresh basil

1 clove garlic, crushed or finely chopped

1 shallot or small onion, grated

¹/₂ tsp Tabasco sauce

2 Tbsp tomato sauce

❖ Soak, cook and drain the beans. Mix all other ingredients and stir into the beans. Serve chilled.

White Bean Bonanza

SERVES 3–4

1 cup dried white beans

2 Tbsp olive oil

1 Tbsp red wine vinegar

2 Tbsp chopped fresh parsley

1 Tbsp chopped chives or garlic greens

2 Tbsp chopped fresh basil

❖ Soak and cook the beans. Drain and purée, adding a little of the cooking liquid. While still warm, beat in the other ingredients. Allow to cool to room temperature.

Serve with green salad.

Variation: If it's too early in the season for fresh basil, 2 Tbsp chopped fresh fennel or chervil leaves are excellent substitutes.

Food for Thought

"The pleasure of eating should be an extensive pleasure, not that of the mere gourmet. People who know the garden in which their vegetables have grown and know that the garden is healthy will remember the beauty of the growing plants, perhaps in the dewy first light of morning when gardens are at their best. Such memory involves itself with the food and is one of the pleasures of eating. The knowledge of the good health of the garden relieves and frees and comforts the eater... A significant part of the pleasure of eating is in one's accurate consciousness of the lives and the world from which food comes. The pleasure of eating, then, may be the best available standard of our health."

— Wendell Berry,
What Are People For?

Garlic's medicinal value is virtually destroyed in cooking, which is why we often add it just before serving a dish, and use it raw in our salad dressings.

Black Bean Delight

SERVES 4

1 cup dried black beans

1 Tbsp cider vinegar or fresh lemon juice

2 Tbsp oil

salt and pepper to taste

1 onion, chopped

2 large tomatoes, chopped

2 cloves garlic, crushed

❖ Soak, cook and drain the beans. Stir in vinegar, oil, salt and pepper while the beans are still warm. Cool and add the onion, tomatoes and garlic. Serve chilled.

Saltspring Three-Bean Salad

SERVES 4–6

¹/₂ cup each of 3 varieties dried beans

¹/₂ cup minced leeks, shallots or chives

6 Tbsp olive oil

2 Tbsp fresh lemon juice

2 Tbsp chopped fresh dill or basil

¹/₂ tsp salt, or to taste

¹/₂ tsp soy sauce

pinch of cayenne pepper

leaves of romaine or other lettuce

lemon and fresh parsley, dill, chervil or chive flowers for garnish

❖ Soak the beans for at least 4 hours. Heat to boiling in separate pots and simmer until desired texture is reached. Drain.

Thoroughly mix all ingredients in a bowl.

Make individual servings by putting ¹/₂ cup or more of the mixture onto a leaf of romaine. Garnish as desired.

Grower's Delight

Most yellow soybeans have a somewhat tinny off-taste. Tiny-seeded Natto soybeans are an exception with their rich pea-like flavour. They are also the best soybeans for sprouting.

Marinated Soybeans

SERVES 4–6

3 cups hot cooked soybeans

³/4 cup oil

¹/3 cup vinegar

salt and pepper to taste

2 cloves garlic, finely chopped

¹/2 cup chopped scallions or chives

¹/2 cup chopped green or red sweet pepper

¹/3 cup chopped celery

2 Tbsp chopped fresh parsley

2 Tbsp chopped fresh dill

❖ Place hot beans in a bowl. Combine oil, vinegar, salt, pepper and garlic, then pour over hot beans. Cover and marinate in the refrigerator several hours.

Stir in scallions, pepper, celery, parsley and dill. Chill again.

Soy and Mushroom Salad

SERVES 4–6

1¹/₂ cups dried soybeans

1 Tbsp oil

1 Tbsp fresh lemon juice

1 clove garlic, crushed

salt and pepper to taste

3 stalks celery, chopped

³/₄ cup sliced mushrooms

4 scallions, finely chopped

❖ Soak and cook the beans, and drain well. Mix together the oil, lemon juice, garlic, salt and pepper. Toss the beans and vegetables in the dressing. Serve chilled.

Food for Thought

"A culture cannot survive long at the expense of either its agricultural or its natural resources. To live at the expense of the source of life is obviously suicidal. Though we have no choice but to live at the expense of other life, it is necessary to recognize the limits and dangers involved: past a certain point in a unified system, 'other life' is our own."

— Wendell Berry, *The Unsettling of America*

Lentil and Rice Salad

SERVES 4–6

2 cups cooked lentils

2 cups cooked rice

1 carrot, grated

³/4 cup chopped leek, kale or garlic greens

❖ Mix all ingredients together and serve with your favourite dressing.

Lively Lentil Lunch

SERVES 4

1¹/4 cups dried lentils

2 Tbsp olive or flax oil

1 Tbsp red wine vinegar

salt and pepper to taste

*2 shallots or mild small onions,
finely chopped*

1 Tbsp Dijon mustard

3 tomatoes, chopped

*1 small red sweet pepper, seeded and
sliced into rings*

¹/4 cucumber, diced

*1 Tbsp finely chopped
fresh parsley or cilantro*

hard-boiled eggs for garnish (optional)

❖ Cook the lentils in unsalted water for 25 minutes, or until tender but not mushy. Drain. While still hot, mix with oil and vinegar. Season with salt and pepper to taste. Stir shallots and mustard into lentils, distributing them evenly. Leave to cool. Stir the vegetables and parsley gently into the salad.

Garnish with sliced hard-boiled eggs if desired.

Sprouted Chick-pea Chow Down

SERVES 4–6

2 cups sprouted chick-peas (see below)

2 cloves garlic, finely chopped

¹/4 cup chopped chives or scallions

1 tomato, diced

¹/4 cup chopped fresh parsley

2 Tbsp red wine vinegar or fresh lemon juice

¹/2 cup olive oil

salt and pepper to taste

salad greens

❖ Combine all ingredients except salad greens, and toss to mix. Serve on a bed of salad greens.

To sprout chick-peas, soak the dried beans overnight in twice their volume of water. Drain. Rinse and drain 2 or 3 times a day until the sprouts are ¹/4–¹/2 inch long. 1 cup dried chick-peas will become 2 cups sprouted chick-peas in about 3 days.

Chick-pea Salad

SERVES 4

1 cup dried chick-peas

3 Tbsp olive oil

1 Tbsp fresh lemon juice

salt and pepper to taste

2 shallots, sliced thin

1 clove garlic, finely chopped

❖ Soak chick-peas and cook until tender. Drain well. Mix together the oil, lemon, salt and pepper. Stir into the warm chick-peas. Cool to room temperature, then add the shallots and garlic.

For a more elaborate version of this salad, see Chick-pea and Feta Feast (following).

"No rational person can see
how using up the topsoil or
the fossil fuels as quickly as
possible can provide greater
security for the future; but
if enough wealth and power
can conjure up the audacity
to say that it can, then sheer
fantasy is given the force of
truth; the future becomes
reckonable as even the past
has never been. It is as if the
future is a newly discovered
continent which the corporations are colonizing.
They have made 'redskins'
of our descendants, holding
them subject to alien val-
ues, while their land is
plundered of anything that
can be shipped home and
sold."
— Wendell Berry, The
Unsettling of America

Chick-pea and Feta Feast

SERVES 4–5

2¹/₂ cups cooked chick-peas

2 large tomatoes, diced

³/₄ cup diced feta cheese

3 shallots, sliced thin

*6–10 olives (your favourite kind),
pitted and quartered*

2 Tbsp chopped fresh parsley

¹/₂ cup light olive oil

*1 Tbsp fresh lemon juice
or red wine vinegar*

1 tsp dried oregano

¹/₂ tsp pepper, or more to taste

❖ Combine chick-peas, tomatoes, cheese, shallots, olives and parsley in a serving bowl. Shake together oil, lemon juice, oregano and pepper in a jar. Pour over salad and toss gently to coat. Serve at room temperature.

Wheatberry Tomato Terrifico

SERVES 6

2 cups cooked wheatberries, cooled

2 cups chopped tomato

¹/₂ cup chopped red onion

¹/₄ cup packed fresh basil leaves, chopped

2 Tbsp olive or flax oil

1 Tbsp red wine vinegar

¹/₂ clove garlic, minced

salt and pepper to taste

❖ In a large bowl, toss together the wheat, tomatoes and onion. Blend the remaining ingredients together. Pour dressing over salad and toss. This salad is best served right after preparation.

Grower's Delight

For those tempted to explore growing, nothing could be finer than to try some fresh herbs or garlic, which can make all the difference in the world to many dishes! We've decreased our salt intake drastically by coming to know the exquisite nuances of fresh herbs—and having twenty-three varieties of garlic to choose from, we're never without a fresh clove!

Sound Nutrition

Sprouted seeds have more vitamin C, B vitamins, protein and iron than most vegetables. They're simple to grow, require moderate care and provide fresh greens rich in live chlorophyll, minerals, vitamins and amino acids throughout the winter months. In addition to the most common sprouts—radish, flax, mustard—try lentils, chick-peas, pinto beans, amaranth and wheat. Seeds increase up to 64 times their volume when sprouted!

Sprouted Wheat Surprise

SERVES 4–5

2 cups sprouted wheatberries (see below)

1 cucumber, peeled and diced

1 yellow, green or red sweet pepper, diced

1 tomato, diced

1 scallion, chopped

1 small celery stalk, diced

2 Tbsp chopped fresh parsley

salt to taste

1/2 cup salad oil

1/2 cup fresh lemon juice

❖ Combine all ingredients in a large bowl. Toss to mix. Cover and refrigerate overnight before serving.

To sprout wheatberries, soak overnight in twice their volume of water. Drain. Rinse and drain 2 or 3 times a day until the sprouts are 1/2 inch long, about 3 days.

Barley and Corn Salad

SERVES 6

3 cups cooked barley

2 cups cooked corn

³/₄ cup diced sweet red pepper

¹/₂ cup diced green pepper

³/₄ cup chopped scallion

¹/₄ cup minced red onion

¹/₄ cup fresh lemon juice

¹/₄ cup olive oil

1 Tbsp minced fresh cilantro

2 Tbsp salt

❖ Combine all ingredients in a large bowl. Marinate 1 hour before serving.

Nutty Quinoa Citrus Salad

SERVES 4

2 cups cooked quinoa, cooled

¹/₂ cup chopped green pepper

¹/₃ cup chopped sweet onion

¹/₂ cup slivered toasted almonds

1 Tbsp olive oil

3 Tbsp orange juice

1 tsp cider vinegar

1 tsp honey

¹/₂ tsp dry mustard

lettuce leaves

2 oranges, sectioned

❖ In a large bowl, toss together quinoa, green pepper, onion and almonds. In a small bowl, stir together oil, juice, vinegar, honey and mustard. Pour dressing over salad and toss until well combined. Line 4 salad bowls with lettuce leaves, top with orange pieces, then top with salad.

Quinoa Hurrah

SERVES 4

2 cups cooked quinoa

1 cup finely diced cucumber

¹/4 cup finely diced scallion

¹/4 cup finely chopped cilantro

3 Tbsp fresh lime or lemon juice

3 Tbsp olive or flax oil

salt and pepper to taste

❖ Combine quinoa, cucumber, scallion and cilantro. Combine lime juice, olive oil and seasonings, pour over salad and toss until thoroughly mixed.

Variation: Add 1 ripe cubed avocado and ¹/3 cup cooked, cooled corn kernels before adding dressing.

Food for Thought

"The existence of so much human hunger in the world is a reality we cannot deny. It is a reality that challenges us deeply: it asks us to become more fully human. The response that each of us makes to the world's hunger is central to the process of our unfolding and growth, essential to the process by which we learn to become more authentic, responsible, and whole human beings. When we try to push the world's hungry away from our minds, we go psychically numb. When we remember those who are without food, something is awakened within us. Our own deeper hungers come to the surface—our hungers to live fully, to bring our lives into alignment with our compassion, to make our lives expressions of our spirits."

—John Robbins, *Diet for a New World*

Quinoa Pear Salad

SERVES 4

1¹/₂ cups quinoa
2 pears, coarsely chopped
¹/₂ cup walnuts, chopped
¹/₄ cup raisins
1 Tbsp olive or flax oil
1 Tbsp honey
1 Tbsp fresh lemon juice
¹/₄ tsp cinnamon
¹/₄ tsp ground ginger
¹/₈ tsp ground nutmeg

❖ Cook and cool the quinoa. In a medium bowl, toss together quinoa, pears, walnuts and raisins. In a small bowl, stir together oil, honey, lemon juice and spices. Pour dressing over salad and toss well.

Zesty Amaranth and Broccoli Salad

SERVES 3–4

This salad works well hot or cold, but we prefer it cold. It's satisfying yet refreshing on a hot summer's day.

1 cup amaranth

2 cups broccoli

2 cloves garlic, minced

1 small onion, sliced

1 orange, sectioned

lettuce leaves and orange slices for garnish

Orange Dressing:

2 cloves garlic, chopped

2 Tbsp rice vinegar

2 Tbsp flax or safflower oil

¹/₄ cup orange juice

1 tsp honey

¹/₂ tsp salt

❖ Cook and cool the amaranth and broccoli. Meanwhile prepare the other ingredients and combine the dressing ingredients. Toss dressing with amaranth, broccoli, garlic, onion and orange sections. Serve on lettuce leaves with orange garnish, if desired.

The Recipes

Hearty Soups

Most all of these soups can be a meal in themselves—great with a hunk of good bread. Soups made with beans and grains are loaded with nutrients, too. A winter soup can't get much heartier than when it's made with beans. In fact, any cooked beans, a few onions and whatever vegetables are in the house will make a soup that satisfies. Try a variety of beans to see how they cook down. Many flavourful beans yield their own delicious broths. Mild beans absorb seasonings and spices well.

Bean soups benefit from a good stock. Some beans render a thick, hearty cooking liquid that we often use as stock, or stock base. The water from steaming vegetables also gives more "essence" of vegetable than commercial bouillons, without sodium or MSG. You can use either bean or vegetable stock or just plain water as the basis for our stock recipes. Vegetable stock is always handy to have in the freezer, and garlic stock is especially wonderful for bean soups.

Prepared in advance, soups can be one helpful item for the busy cook to have on hand. Plus beans and grains are so versatile in soups that taking whatever ingredients you happen to have on hand can be a fast way out of the "What am I going to have for dinner?" dilemma. May these recipes inspire your natural ingenuity!

Vegetable Stock

We keep a container in the fridge to collect the tops and bottoms of celery, carrots, parsnips, potatoes, leeks and the skins of onion or garlic for this stock. Brassicas such as cabbage and broccoli tend to dominate, so use them sparingly.

1–1$^1/_2$ cups chopped vegetables

4 cups water

1 bay leaf

$^1/_2$ strip kombu or other seaweed (or $^1/_2$ tsp salt to taste)

❖ Bring all ingredients to a boil over medium-high heat, then simmer uncovered for a couple of hours. Strain before using. Keep the stock in the refrigerator or freezer unless using it the same day.

Garlic Stock

MAKES 4 CUPS

2 garlic bulbs

3 cups water

1 cup chopped vegetables

2 sprigs fresh parsley

1 bay leaf

❖ Separate the garlic bulbs into cloves, but don't peel them. Place the cloves in a large saucepan with the water, vegetables, parsley and bay leaf. Bring to a boil over high heat, then simmer 2 hours. Strain. Keep the stock in the refrigerator or freezer unless using it the same day.

Black Bean Soup

SERVES 6–8

Ground cumin, an important ingredient in this soup, is a great seasoning for black beans in any form.

2 cups dried black beans

10 cups stock

1 large onion, chopped

3 cloves garlic, minced

2 carrots, finely grated

2 stalks celery, finely chopped

3 Tbsp dried parsley

3 Tbsp unsulphured molasses

2–3 Tbsp soy sauce

1–2 Tbsp oil

2 tsp ground cumin

1 tsp salt

$^1/_2$ tsp ground cloves

several dashes sea kelp

cayenne pepper to taste

chopped fresh parsley, scallions, alfalfa sprouts or chives for garnish

❖ Soak the beans and cook them in the stock. Sauté onion, garlic, carrrots, celery and parsley until very tender. Add to beans with remaining ingredients. Cook everything together for 15–20 minutes. Correct seasonings. Garnish as desired.

Pesto Pizzazz

SERVES 4–6

Pesto is handy to have on hand for adding to bean soups. Or, make it up while the soup thickens!

¹/₂ cup kidney, pinto or other mild-flavoured dried beans, soaked

4 cups water

1 onion, chopped

1 Tbsp olive oil

3 tomatoes chopped

3 carrots, diced

1 leek, chopped

1 stalk celery with leaves, chopped

2 potatoes, diced

salt and pepper to taste

2 zucchini, diced

1 cup green beans, sliced

¹/₄ cup broken spaghetti

Pesto:

3 cloves garlic

2 Tbsp chopped fresh basil

3 tsp tomato paste

Did You Know . . . ?

A 1991 Gallup poll conducted for the National Restaurant Association concluded that about 20 percent of people look for vegetarian items when they eat out. A third of us would order non-meat items if offered.

¹/₂ cup freshly grated Parmesan cheese

2 Tbsp olive oil

❖ Cook the beans in the water. Drain and reserve liquid. Cook onion in oil until soft. Add tomatoes and cook for 2 minutes, while stirring. Add half the bean liquid, the carrots, leeks, celery, potatoes, salt and pepper. Bring to a boil and simmer 10–15 minutes.

Add zucchini, green beans and remaining bean liquid. Cook 5 more minutes. Bring to a full boil and add spaghetti. Lower heat and simmer 15 minutes.

Meanwhile, prepare the pesto. With a mortar and pestle or in a blender or food processor, crush the garlic and basil together to a green paste. Blend in tomato paste and cheese. Add oil slowly until a thick paste results. Thin with 2 Tbsp of the stock. Serve in separate bowl so diners can add pesto as they like.

Kale and Bean Soup

SERVES 4–6

Green leafy vegetables are great additions to bean soups. For this one, we prefer kale or amaranth greens, but chard, endive and quinoa greens can be used too.

2 cups stock

2 cups water

2 Tbsp thinly sliced garlic

1–1¹/₂ pounds green leafy vegetables

2 cups cooked beans

3 Tbsp olive oil

¹/₂ tsp pepper

2 eggs, beaten

lemon wedges and freshly grated Parmesan cheese (optional)

❖ In a large saucepan, bring stock and water to boil. Add garlic and kale, stirring to submerge. Cover and cook about 5 minutes. Add the beans, oil and pepper, stirring occasionally for a few minutes until beans are heated through.

Stirring gently, pour the beaten eggs in a stream into the saucepan to form thin strands. Serve hot. Top each bowl with a lemon wedge and serve with grated Parmesan if desired.

Iron deficiency affects about 10 percent of the North American population, but those on diets rich in dried beans and dark green leafy vegetables have less chance of being counted in this group.

Gwen Mallard's Pea Soup

SERVES 8

1/2 cup barley

2 cups dried soup peas

2 Tbsp olive oil

salt to taste

12 cups boiling water

1 large onion, chopped

1/4 medium cabbage, chopped

2 medium potatoes, diced

2 large carrots, diced

chopped fresh herbs to taste

❖ Place barley, peas, oil and salt in a large pot. Pour boiling water over ingredients and simmer gently, stirring frequently to prevent sticking. Cook about 2 hours or until peas are at the purée stage. Add vegetables and cook slowly until tender without overcooking. Add salt and favourite herbs. This soup thickens as it stands and requires water when reheated.

Soybean Soup

SERVES 6

1 1/2 cups soybeans

1/4 cup water

2 onions, chopped

2 cloves garlic, chopped

2 Tbsp oil

2 celery stalks, diced

1 green pepper, diced

2 carrots, diced

2 cups canned tomatoes
(or fresh, skinned and chopped)

4 cups Vegetable Stock or water

1/2 tsp dried thyme or savory

2 Tbsp chopped fresh parsley

salt to taste

❖ Cook the soybeans. Place half of them in a blender with 1/4 cup water and blend until smooth. Sauté onions and garlic in oil until tender. Add celery, green pepper and carrots, then cook 5 minutes longer, stirring occasionally.

Add tomatoes, stock, thyme, parsley, salt and blended beans. Bring to a boil, cover and simmer gently until vegetables are crisp-tender.

Add remaining whole soybeans and reheat.

Did You Know . . . ?

An acre of land can produce about 165 pounds of beef, whereas the same acre could produce 2,000 pounds of soybeans; the production of 1 pound of beef requires 2,500 gallons of water, compared to 25 gallons for the same amount of quinoa. As of 1974, the livestock population of the US was consuming enough grain and soybeans to feed the global population five times over.

Grower's Delight

Some soup pea varieties have pretty pink and purple flowers followed by stunning purple pods. Two of the best-tasting of these are Blue Pod Désirée and Tall Capucijners.

Legume Triple Treat

SERVES 8

2 cups dried soup beans, soaked

1 cup dried Capucijner or other soup peas, soaked

1 cup lentils

12 cups boiling water

1 large onion, chopped

2 cups kale, amaranth or cabbage greens

2 large carrots, sliced

salt and pepper to taste

❖ Place beans, peas, lentils and water in a large pot. Simmer until beans are tender. Add vegetables and simmer 20 minutes longer. Add salt, pepper or other seasonings to taste.

When reheating, add water.

Variation: Substitute 1 cup fava beans for 1 cup of the soup beans and add 1 cup fresh corn kernels.

Kevin's Soybean and Sunroot Chowder

SERVES 7-10

Sunroots have a unique sweet, nutty taste and crisp texture. They make a delicious cream soup on their own, and a fine addition to any soup.

3 cups cooked soybeans

4 cups cold water

2 tsp salt

$^1/_2$ tsp pepper

1 bay leaf

2 cups stewed chopped tomatoes

2 cups peeled, diced sunroot

2 cups chopped carrots

1 cup chopped onion

$^1/_2$ cup chopped green pepper

$1^1/_2$ cups milk

❖ In a large stock pot, combine soybeans, cold water, salt, pepper and bay leaf. Cover and bring to a full boil. Reduce heat and simmer for 1–1$^1/_2$ hours. Add tomatoes, sunroot, carrots, onion and green pepper. Cover and simmer 30 minutes longer or until vegetables are soft. Stir in milk and serve with large chunks of multi-grain bread.

Did You Know . . . ?

Early in the seventeenth century, the "sunroots" that Samuel de Champlain found North American natives eating became a staple winter food for early settlers, but also gained quick popularity in Europe. Its cultivation as a food crop throughout the western world faded, except in England, with the widespread introduction of potatoes in the following century.

This plant is also known as "Jerusalem artichoke." It is thought that "Jerusalem" is a corruption of the Italian name for the plant "girasole," which refers to the plant's habit of turning its tall, sunflower-topped stalks toward the sun. The word "artichoke" was likely introduced because of the tuber's similarity in taste to globe artichokes. But since it is neither from Jerusalem nor an artichoke, but a second cousin to the sunflower, we prefer to call it "sunroot."

Note

To prepare sunroots, clean them with a stiff brush under running water. Knobby parts can be cut to get into crevices if desired, but peeling is unnecessary. Because they discolour quickly, like apples, rub them with lemon juice or place them in cold water to which lemon juice or vinegar has been added, especially if there is a time gap between preparation and eating or cooking.

Sunroots can be eaten raw, alone or in salads. They can be steamed, sautéed or stir-fried, and cooked in most ways potatoes are prepared. Unlike potatoes, though, they lose a lot of their appeal when overcooked.

Sound Nutrition

Sunroots store carbohydrates in the form of inulin instead of starch. As with most fruits, their sugars are stored as levulose. For these reasons, and because they have only one-tenth the calories of white potatoes, they are often recommended for diabetics or anyone who needs to watch starch or calorie consumption.

A tip from Kevin: "On the first night it tastes great, but heated up as leftovers, after the flavours have had a chance to marry overnight in the refrigerator, it tastes superb!"

Fava Bean Soup

SERVES 3–4

1 large onion, chopped

2 cloves garlic, minced

1 carrot, grated

3 Tbsp oil

4 cups cooked favas

1/2 cup tomato sauce

1/2 cup plain yogurt

seasonings to taste

❖ Sauté onion, garlic and carrot in oil. Add favas and other ingredients and purée in blender, adding more water or tomato sauce if necessary. Reheat without boiling.

Grower's Delight

Cambridge Scarlet favas have a very attractive, long-lasting scarlet flower that contrasts with its grey green leaves. They are one of the few favas that are excellent either fresh or dried.

Growers' Delight

The Bell or Tic Bean is our favourite small-seeded fava. The outer skin has a pleasant chewiness and the inside tastes like new potatoes. Many of the larger favas are tough and bland when cooked after being dried, but both the Purple and Aprovecho varieties are tasteful and satisfying.

Fasalada Sopa

SERVES 3–4

1 onion, sliced

2 cloves garlic, finely chopped

3 Tbsp olive oil

1 Tbsp tomato paste

¹/₂ tsp dried thyme

1 cup dried fava beans, soaked

juice of 1 lemon

handful of chopped fresh parsley

❖ Cook the onion and garlic gently in the oil until soft but not brown. Stir in the tomato paste and thyme. Add the beans and cook for 1 hour in enough water to cover by 1 inch. Sieve the mixture coarsely or purée in a blender at slow speed. Stir in the lemon juice and parsley. Serve hot.

Merry Minestrone with Chick-peas

SERVES 6–8

1 cup diced onion or leek

³/₄ cup diced celery

2 cloves garlic, minced

¹/₄ cup olive oil

3¹/₂ cups tomato juice

3 bay leaves

1 Tbsp honey or rice syrup

1 Tbsp cider vinegar

1 tsp salt

1 cup skinned and chopped tomato

³/₄ cup diced carrot

³/₄ cup diced parsnip

³/₄ cup cauliflower florets

¹/₂ cup diced zucchini or small zucchini
cut in rounds

¹/₂ cup halved green beans

³/₄ cup stemmed and shredded kale,
amaranth or spinach greens

1 cup cooked chick-peas

1 cup uncooked shell pasta or macaroni

1–2 cups water or stock

1/4 cup minced fresh basil

1 Tbsp minced fresh rosemary

1/3 cup fresh Italian parsley

1/4 cup minced fresh mint

❖ In a heavy-bottomed pan, sauté onion, celery and garlic in oil. Add tomato juice, bay leaves, honey, vinegar and salt. Bring to a simmer over medium heat. Add the vegetables to the pot and simmer, uncovered, 10 minutes. Add chick-peas, pasta and water or stock as needed. Simmer until pasta is tender. Add herbs to soup for last 5 minutes of cooking. Serve hot.

Variation: Try different vegetables, such as broccoli, green or red sweet pepper, etc.

Lentil Soup

SERVES 4–6

3 cloves garlic, finely chopped

1 large onion, chopped

1 celery stalk, chopped

$^1/_4$ cup celery leaves or
1 Tbsp lovage leaves

2 carrots, sliced thick

3 Tbsp oil or butter

$1^1/_2$ cups dried lentils

$^1/_3$ cup barley or brown rice

2 Tbsp chopped fresh parsley

3 Tbsp brewer's yeast

5 whole cloves (optional)

❖ Sauté vegetables in oil until fragrant. Add lentils, cloves, barley, parsley, brewer's yeast and enough water to cover by 3 inches. Simmer, covered, for 45–60 minutes.

Variation: For a richer, more robust soup, add 1 cup shredded green leafy vegetables such as collards, kale, spinach or beet greens; and add 1–2 Tbsp miso just before serving.

Chick-pea Gazpacho

SERVES 8

1 cup cooked chick-peas

4 cups vegetable cocktail juice

3 cups diced tomato

1/2 cup diced green pepper

1/2 cup cooked corn

1/2 cup diced cucumber

1/4 cup minced red onion

1/4 cup chopped fresh parsley

2 Tbsp lime juice

2 Tbsp rice vinegar

1 tsp honey

1 tsp Vegit, Spike, etc.

1/2 tsp pepper

1 clove garlic, minced

1/4 tsp cayenne pepper

❖ Mix all ingredients together in a large bowl and chill overnight. Serve cold.

Ginger Barley Soup

SERVES 3–4

1 onion, chopped

1" knob of fresh ginger, grated

2 Tbsp oil

1 carrot, diced

1 parsnip, diced

3 tomatoes, chopped

¹/₂ cup barley

5 cups Vegetable Stock

salt and pepper to taste

minced fresh parsley for garnish

❖ Sauté onion and ginger in oil for 5 minutes. Stir in carrot and parsnip and sauté 5 minutes more. Add the tomatoes and barley. Combine with the stock in soup pot and simmer for about 1 hour. Add the salt and pepper near the end. Garnish with minced parsley.

Variation: For a fuller-bodied soup, add ¹/₂ cup soup peas with the barley.

The Physicians Committee for Responsible Medicine has proposed that recommended food groups be amended, from meat and dairy to the following:

- *Whole grains (5 or more servings daily)*

- *Legumes (2 or 3 servings daily)*

- *Vegetables (3 or more servings daily)*

- *Fruits (3 or more servings daily)*

Our opinion is that these quantities may be necessary for those who eat refined grains only, and are probably excessive for those who eat whole grains.

Quinoa Chowder

SERVES 3–4

3 cups water

¹/₂ cup quinoa

1 medium potato, cubed

1 medium carrot, sliced

1 celery stalk, sliced

1 medium onion, chopped

¹/₂ cup dried lentils

3 cloves garlic, minced

1 cup corn kernels

2 cups milk

1 cup grated cheese

❖ Simmer everything except the milk and cheese for 30 minutes. Add milk and cheese. Bring to a low simmer, season to taste and serve.

Barley Bean Soup

SERVES 3–4

1 onion, sliced

2 Tbsp butter

1 celery stalk, diced

2 carrots, diced

3 cups water or stock

1 cup dried beans, soaked

2–3 Tbsp barley

1 Tbsp dried crushed herbs

salt and pepper to taste

❖ Cook the onion in the butter over medium heat until lightly browned. Add the celery and carrot. Cover with the stock and add the beans and barley. Bring to the boil, then simmer 50 minutes. Add the seasonings and simmer 30 minutes longer.

Variation: A few cloves of garlic, sautéed along with the other vegetables, impart a nice flavour to this soup. Garnish with finely chopped chervil.

Grower's Delight

Many of the large baking beans that have been part of northeast American cuisine for hundreds of years are also great soup beans. Jacob's Cattle, Maine Yellow Eye and Soldier Bean are heirlooms with a mild taste and a wonderful capacity to absorb spices and seasonings.

Did You Know . . . ?

Garlic is a member of the lily family and is related to onions and shallots.

Garlic Soup

SERVES 4–6

2 garlic bulbs, separated into cloves, peeled and chopped

1 large onion, minced

3 Tbsp olive oil

4 cups tomatoes, peeled and chopped

2 tsp minced fresh basil

¹/₂ tsp minced fresh tarragon

4 cups Vegetable Stock or water

salt and pepper to taste

❖ Sauté garlic and onions in oil in a soup pot over medium heat, being careful not to brown them. When they are translucent, add the chopped tomato, basil and tarragon, then stir for 2 minutes. Add the stock, bring to a boil, then reduce to a simmer. Cook about 45 minutes. Add salt and pepper.

Variation: To make a more substantial soup, add leftover cooked rice or pasta just before serving.

The Main Course

This section offers a range of main course dishes calling for plant proteins and a variety of vegetables. Yes, having to soak most legumes requires some thinking ahead, but the simmering itself requires little tending, and preparing fresh, whole ingredients is surprisingly easy and quick.

But in our fast-paced culture, where fast foods are the norm, we can't stress strongly enough the importance of savouring these meals. They are anything but "fast foods"— beans and grains might more appropriately be called "slow" foods. It's really difficult to gulp down a bowl of barley pilaf. By their very nature, these foods persuade you to savour every mouthful. They seduce you with their pleasant persistence and make a meal long and luxurious.

Helen Nearing, in her book *Simple Food for the Good Life*, suggests: "I believe the work of feeding people could be simplified to such a point that it would take less time to prepare a meal than to eat it, whereas now it is usually the other way around. Perhaps that might be the test for rational eating. If you eat for half an hour, or an hour, put only that much (or less) time into preparation; no more. Then you would be closer to living simply on simple food."

May these main courses provide simple food, simply prepared, to nourish you and your loved ones!

The Recipes

Italian Bean Stew

SERVES 2–4

1 cup dried white beans

1 onion, chopped

2 cloves garlic, chopped or minced

2 Tbsp oil

4 large tomatoes, chopped

1 tsp dried oregano

1¹/₂ tsp chopped fresh basil

1 bay leaf

1 tsp molasses

salt and pepper to taste

❖ Soak, cook and drain the beans. Cook onion and garlic in oil over medium-high heat until soft but not brown. Add remaining ingredients, bring to the boil, then simmer 20 minutes. Stir the drained beans into the vegetables, bring to the boil and serve in bowls.

Black Beans with Tomatoes and Cilantro

SERVES 2–4

1 cup dried black beans, soaked

1 onion, chopped

2 cloves garlic, chopped

1¹/₂ Tbsp oil

6 tomatoes, chopped

¹/₂ tsp Tabasco sauce

salt to taste

2 Tbsp chopped fresh cilantro

❖ Cook and drain the beans. Sauté onion and garlic in oil over medium-high heat until onion is almost translucent but still firm. Add tomatoes and cook several minutes longer. Add and combine beans, Tabasco and salt. Cover and cook 2–3 minutes, or until beans are heated through. Remove from heat and stir in half the cilantro. Transfer to a serving dish and sprinkle with remaining cilantro.

Sound Nutrition

Beans have many factors in their favour. They are one of the five least allergenic foods. They are high in protein and are well-endowed with thiamine, niacin, vitamin B6 and folic acid as well as calcium, iron, phosphorus and potassium. The fibre in beans helps keep the digestive system clean and promotes regularity.

Black Bean Bash

SERVES 6–8

2 cups dried black beans

2 cups brown rice

1/4 cup oil

1 onion, finely chopped

2 cloves garlic, finely chopped

2 tsp ground cumin

2–4 tomatoes, coarsely chopped

salt and pepper to taste

❖ Cook the beans and rice. Heat oil in a skillet over medium-high heat. Add onion, garlic and cumin and sauté, stirring frequently, until onion is translucent. Add tomatoes and cook 3–4 minutes, stirring until well blended. Season. Turn heat to low. Stir in beans and cover, simmering gently for 15 minutes. Mound hot cooked rice on serving plate and create a well in the centre for the beans.

Rice and Red Beans

SERVES 6–8

2 cups dried red kidney beans

2 cups brown rice

1 large onion, chopped

1–2 carrots, chopped

1 celery stalk or 1 sweet pepper, chopped

2/3 cup chopped fresh parsley

2–3 tsp chopped fresh basil

2 tsp dried oregano

2 Tbsp oil

2–3 tomatoes, chopped

salt and pepper to taste

*grated cheese and fresh parsley
for garnish*

❖ Cook beans and rice. Sauté onion, carrots, celery, the 2/3 cup parsley, basil and oregano in oil. Add tomatoes, salt, pepper and beans. Mix in rice and make sure all is heated through.

Garnish with grated cheese and more fresh parsley, if desired.

Food for Thought

"Only by restoring the broken connections can we be healed. Connection is health. And what our society does its best to disguise from us is how ordinary, how commonly attainable, health is. We lose our health—and create profitable diseases and dependencies—by failing to see the direct connections between living and eating, eating and working, working and loving. In gardening, for instance, one works with the body to feed the body. The work, if it is knowledgeable, makes for excellent food. And it makes one hungry. The work thus makes eating both nourishing and joyful, not consumptive, and keeps the eater from getting fat and weak. This is health, wholeness, a source of delight. And such a solution, unlike the typical industrial solution, does not cause new problems.

"The 'drudgery' of growing one's own food, then, is not drudgery at all. (If we make the growing of food a drudgery, which is what 'agribusiness' does make of it, then we also make a drudgery of eating and of living.) It is—in addition to being the appropriate fulfillment of a prac-

Blast o' Pasta

SERVES 4–6

1 cup chopped onion

1¹/₂ cups chopped tomato

3 cloves garlic, minced

1 Tbsp olive oil

2 cups cooked beans, drained

2 cups cooked elbow macaroni

¹/₂ cup minced fresh parsley

1 tsp dried oregano

¹/₂ tsp dried basil

salt and pepper to taste

❖ In a large skillet over medium-high heat, sauté the onions, tomatoes and garlic in the oil. Add the beans, pasta, parsley, oregano and basil. Heat through. Season.

Vegetarian Chili

SERVES 6

1¹/₂ cups dried kidney or pinto beans

1 onion, sliced thin

2–4 cloves garlic, chopped

2 celery stalks, chopped

3 tomatoes, chopped

3 Tbsp oil

1¹/₂ cups stock or bean cooking liquid

1 tsp ground cumin

1 dried hot chili or 3 Tbsp chili powder

1 tsp soy sauce

1 tsp cayenne pepper

salt and pepper to taste

❖ Cook and drain the beans. Sauté vegetables lightly in oil. Combine with beans, stock and seasonings. Bring to a boil and then simmer, covered, for at least 1 hour.

Variation: Add any combination of ¹/₄ cup tomato paste, sliced mushrooms, chutney or corn kernels.

Soy and Peas Please

SERVES 4

1 cup soybeans, soaked

1 sweet onion, sliced thin

1 1/4 cups green peas, fresh or frozen

2 Tbsp olive oil

2 Tbsp red or white wine vinegar

salt and pepper to taste

❖ Cook the soybeans. Drain well and add onion and peas. Mix oil, vinegar, salt and pepper and stir into the beans while still warm. Seve chilled.

Variation: Extend this dish by adding crisp lettuce leaves, sliced tomatoes and diced cucumber. Lima beans work as well as the soybeans.

Soybean and Rice Curry

SERVES 4

2 medium onions, chopped

3 Tbsp butter or oil

3 Tbsp soy sauce

2 Tbsp nutritional yeast

1–2 tsp curry powder, or to taste

3/4 cup cooked brown rice

1 1/2 cups cooked soybeans

❖ Sauté onions in butter. Mix with soy sauce, yeast and curry powder. Combine rice, beans and sauce. Stir well until heated through.

Sound Nutrition

Soybeans not only have the highest protein content of all legumes, but they are considered to be a "complete protein" food. With a wealth of beans available, whole or natural food proponents no longer have to rely so heavily on processed soy products such as tofu, tempeh, soy milk and miso.

Fava Stew

SERVES 5–6

1/4 cup butter or oil

1 large onion, chopped

1/2 cup grated carrot

1 celery stalk, diced

2 cloves garlic, minced

1/2 cup all-purpose flour

1/4 tsp dried thyme

salt and pepper to taste

pinch of nutmeg

1 cup Vegetable Stock or Garlic Stock

2 eggs, well beaten

1/2 cup fresh French sorrel

1/2 cup kale, chopped fine

4 cups cooked favas

❖ Heat butter and sauté onion, carrot, celery and garlic 5–8 minutes. Stir in flour, thyme, salt, pepper and nutmeg. Gradually add stock and cook, stirring gently, for 10 minutes. Turn heat down and stir in eggs slowly. Cook a few more minutes and add sorrel, kale and cooked favas. Heat through and serve.

Sweet and Sour Lentils

SERVES 4

2 cups Vegetable Stock

1 cup dried lentils

1 bay leaf

salt to taste

1 clove garlic, finely chopped

1/8 tsp ground cloves

1/8 tsp nutmeg

3 Tbsp oil

3 Tbsp apple cider or juice

3 Tbsp cider vinegar

3 Tbsp honey, molasses or sugar

❖ Bring the stock to a boil in a large pot and add the lentils, bay leaf and salt. Cover and simmer gently for 30 minutes. Add remaining ingredients. Stir to mix well. Cook 5 minutes longer, or until lentils are tender.

Did You Know . . . ?

Lentils have been cultivated for 10,000 or more years. Lens is the Latin word for lentil, so named because of its doubly convex shape. Lentils are an enormously important staple food in many countries, especially in Asia and North Africa.

Lentil Pumpkin Pleasure

SERVES 4–6

1 medium onion, finely chopped

2 Tbsp butter or oil

1 cup dried lentils

3 cups cubed fresh pumpkin

1 Tbsp fresh lemon juice

2 Tbsp chopped fresh parsley

salt and pepper to taste

¹/₂ tsp ground ginger

¹/₂ tsp ground cumin

❖ In a large saucepan, sauté onion in butter until just golden. Add lentils and combine to coat with butter. Cover barely with cold water. Turn heat to medium-high and bring to a boil. Reduce to a simmer and cook, covered, stirring occasionally until lentils are barely tender.

Add remaining ingredients. Stir well to mix, cover and cook 20–30 minutes, or until pumpkin is tender.

Barley and Vegetable Mélange

SERVES 4

2 carrots, chopped

1 onion, chopped

1 potato, diced

1 small parsnip or turnip, chopped

1 cup shredded cabbage

$^1/_2$ cup barley

1 tsp salt

$2^1/_2$ cups stock or water

❖ Place all ingredients in a heavy casserole. Bring to a boil, cover and simmer 50 minutes.

Lentil and Amaranth Stew

SERVES 5–6

1¹/₂–2 cups amaranth leaves, coarsely chopped

2 cups dried lentils, cooked and drained

1 tsp ground cumin

1 tsp ground coriander

2 cloves garlic, finely chopped

salt and pepper to taste

❖ Steam amaranth greens gently for 5–6 minutes. Drain. Stir in lentils, spices, garlic, amaranth greens and season to taste.

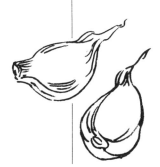

Amaranth or Quinoa Lasagna

SERVES 5–6

Because of the high protein content of amaranth and quinoa, this lasagna is more filling than regular lasagnas. Good all year round and especially satisfying in winter.

Sauce:

1¹/₂ cups tomato sauce

2 cups chopped tomato

¹/₂ cup tomato paste

1 cup water

¹/₂ cup chopped celery

1 cup sliced mushrooms

1 onion, chopped

1 cup lentils

1 carrot, grated

1 tsp dried oregano

1 tsp dried basil

1 tsp Spike, Vegit, etc.

3–4 cloves garlic, finely chopped

¹/₂ tsp cayenne pepper

1¹/₂ cups amaranth or quinoa

Did You Know . . . ?

whole wheat or spinach lasagna noodles, cooked

1 cup cottage cheese

1 cup quinoa or amaranth greens, chopped

1¹/₂ cups mozzarella or Monterey jack cheese, grated

❖ Combine sauce ingredients, adding amaranth last, and simmer 30–60 minutes. Add more water or tomato sauce if necessary.

Preheat oven to 350°F. Spread a third of the noodles in a large baking pan. Cover with a third of the cottage cheese, then a third of the greens, then a third of the sauce. Repeat twice, then top with grated cheese. Bake 30 minutes.

Amaranth Stir-Fry

SERVES 4

1 celery stalk, sliced

1 cup sliced mushrooms

1 carrot, sliced

1 onion, chopped

3 cloves garlic, finely chopped

$^1/_2$ cup almonds, chopped

$^1/_4$ cup sunflower seeds

2 Tbsp oil

2 Tbsp soy sauce

1 tsp kelp flakes, Spike, etc.

2 cups cooked amaranth

❖ Sauté vegtables, garlic, almonds and seeds in oil until vegetables are tender-crisp. Add seasonings and amaranth. Mix well until warm through.

Variation: Quinoa works as well as amaranth.

Baby Beans and Quinoa

SERVES 4–5

1 cup quinoa

¹/₂ cup chopped onion

¹/₂ cup chopped green pepper

1 Tbsp oil

1 cup water

1 cup small dried beans, cooked

2 Tbsp chopped fresh cilantro

¹/₄ tsp cayenne or chili pepper

❖ Cook the quinoa as directed on page 54. At the same time, in a large saucepan, sauté onion and pepper in the oil until softened.

Stir in water and bring to a boil. Stir in beans, then the cooked quinoa. Lower the heat, cover and simmer 10 more minutes. Remove from heat and stir in cilantro and pepper.

Quinoa Stew

SERVES 3–4

2 Tbsp oil

1/2 cup quinoa

1 onion, chopped

2 cloves garlic, finely chopped

1 cup tomato sauce

1 cup corn kernels

1/2 tsp ground cumin

1/4 tsp cayenne pepper

grated cheese (optional)

❖ In a large saucepan, heat oil over medium-high heat. Add quinoa, onion and garlic. Stir until quinoa starts to crackle and onion is softened. Add tomato sauce, corn, cumin and cayenne. Bring to a boil, then simmer, covered, for 20 minutes. Remove from heat and let stand 5 minutes. Sprinkle with grated cheese before serving, if desired.

Sound Nutrition

The protein in quinoa and amaranth has an essential amino acid balance close to the ideal. In fact, both grains come closer to meeting the ideal protein requirements of the human body than either cow's milk or soybeans. They are high in the amino acid lysine, which is lacking in most cereals such as wheat, sorghum, corn and barley. Relatively small amounts of amaranth or quinoa provide complete protein. Many health food stores now carry the flours from these grains, and bulk food stores should follow soon.

Casseroles, Loaves and Burgers

Many of these recipes are great for using up leftover beans. Cook up an extra cup or two to have on hand now and then, or pre-prepare a batch of burgers or a loaf to have in the freezer for an easy meal. Many of these recipes are "meals in a dish," mélanges of beans or grains with a range of vegetables and seasonings. Mixing all that food together, we become aware of how many plants are included in a given meal . . .

We are blessed with being able to pick our food just before preparing or cooking it. Our time in the garden is nourishing. Moving from garden to kitchen to table helps us stay connected to the source of our food, with gratitude. Even if you don't grow your own, try making a mental connection to the source of each food you use—the live plant or animal. See yourself receiving the full benefit of that life energy, and the combined energies of the plants, as you eat.

Bean-Rice Squares

SERVES 4

2 cups cooked beans

1 egg, beaten

1 cup milk

¹/₂ tsp salt

1 tsp Worcestershire sauce

¹/₂ teaspoon dry mustard

¹/₄ cup sliced scallions

1 cup cooked brown rice

1¹/₂ cups grated cheese
(Swiss, cheddar or a combination)

❖ Preheat oven to 325°F. Mix the cooked beans with all the other ingredients and pour into a well-greased 8-inch square baking pan. Bake 40–50 minutes. The mixture should be just set, like a custard, but not dried out.

Did You Know . . . ?

Bean varieties are often named after the specific person who discovered and/ or popularized them. Some examples are Aunt Jean's, Low's Champion, Uncle Willie's, Gramma Walters, Bill Jump's.

Apple-Tomato Bake

SERVES 4

1 cup white beans (Great Northern, white kidney or cannellini)

2 Tbsp oil

1 large onion, sliced

1 large apple, seeded and sliced

2–3 Tbsp maple syrup

¹/₄ cup tomato paste

❖ Preheat oven to 300°F. Combine all ingredients in a casserole, cover and bake 2 hours. Stir gently every half hour. To reduce liquid, if desired, leave uncovered during the last half hour.

Black Bean Burgers

SERVES 4

2 cups dried black beans, cooked and drained

¹/₃ cup finely chopped onion

¹/₄ cup finely chopped sweet red pepper

1 Tbsp diced green chili peppers

1 tsp ground cumin

3 Tbsp toasted seeds (sesame and/or pumpkin and/or sunflower

salt and pepper to taste

2 Tbsp oil

4 burger buns

cheese, lettuce, tomato, pickles, masala, etc. for garnish

❖ In a medium bowl, mash the beans with a fork until smooth, leaving some of them intact. Add onion, pepper, chilies, cumin, seeds and seasoning. Mix well. Divide mixture into 4 even parts and form by hand into large flat patties.

Heat oil in a skillet over medium heat. Fry the burgers on one side until brown. Turn the burgers over with a large spatula and do the other side. Serve on open-face buns and garnish as desired.

Many bean names indicate their heirloom nature. Some, such as Arikara, Nez Perce and Anasazi have been grown in North America for hundreds of years.

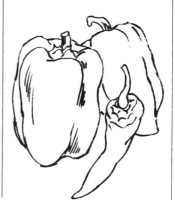

Grower's Delight

Grand Forks soybeans have a two-tone yellow and brown pattern that makes them look like kids' candies. They cook to a rich, robust and buttery flavour.

Soybean Casserole

SERVES 2–4

Soybeans benefit from other strong flavours, so go ahead and add your favourite pungent herbs to this dish.

1 cup soybeans

1 onion, chopped

2 cloves garlic, finely chopped or crushed

1 celery stalk, chopped

3 tomatoes, chopped

2 Tbsp butter or oil

2 Tbsp chopped fresh parsley

2–4 Tbsp chopped fresh herbs (basil, chives, oregano, celery leaves and/or lemon thyme)

salt and pepper to taste

water or stock

❖ Cook the soybeans. Meanwhile, preheat oven to 350°F. Cook onion, garlic and vegetables in butter for about 8 minutes until soft. Stir in herbs and seasonings.

Put drained beans in oven casserole and stir in vegetable mixture. Barely cover with water or stock, cover and bake 1 hour.

Soybean Loaf

SERVES 4

2 1/2 cups cooked soybeans

1 cup cooked rice or other grain

1/4 cup sesame, almond or peanut butter

1/4 cup wheat germ

1 tomato, finely chopped

1 cup grated carrot

1 onion, finely chopped

2 cloves garlic, minced fine

2 Tbsp oil

1 tsp salt

1/2 tsp dried tarragon

❖ Preheat oven to 350°F. Mash the soybeans. Combine all ingredients in a casserole dish and bake, uncovered, 45 minutes.

Did You Know . . . ?

Commercial soybeans are relatively free of chemical toxins. Meat, fish and poultry have about twenty times and dairy foods about four and one half times more pesticide residues than soybeans. Similarly, soybeans contain fewer radioactive residues and no synthetic hormones.

Soy-Grain Burgers

SERVES 4

1 1/2 cups soybeans

1 cup cooked millet or brown rice

2 Tbsp chopped onion

2 eggs, lightly beaten

1 tsp salt

1 cup whole wheat bread crumbs

1/4 tsp paprika

2 Tbsp chopped fresh parsley

1/2 cup wheat germ

❖ Cook soybeans until soft. Preheat oven to 350°F, or heat broiler. Mash soybeans and mix with all ingredients except the wheat germ. Form into 4 patties and roll them in the wheat germ. Broil until lightly browned or bake on baking sheet for 35 minutes.

Variation: Add other seasonings for more exciting tastes: chopped celery or lovage leaves, cumin, sage, thyme, garlic, mustard.

Soy Nut Burgers

SERVES 4–5

1 cup cooked soybeans

^{1}/2 cup peanuts

^{1}/2 cup cashews or sunflower seeds, roasted (optional)

3 Tbsp tomato paste

1 onion, chopped

^{1}/2 tsp chili powder or chopped chili pepper

^{1}/4 cup chopped fresh parsley

1 egg, beaten

^{1}/4 cup water, or more for consistency

2 Tbsp sesame seeds

bread crumbs or wheat germ for coating

❖ Mash soybeans. Preheat oven to 350°F.

Process all ingredients except soybeans, sesame seeds and bread crumbs in blender, leaving some pieces for texture. Remove from blender and stir in beans and sesame seeds. Mold into 4 or 5 burgers, roll in bread crumbs and bake 40 minutes on a baking sheet.

Serve as is, or in whole wheat buns or pita bread, with lettuce and tomato, shredded cabbage, guacamole, salsa, etc.

Did You Know . . . ?

Most people on this continent have yet to discover the excellence of unadulterated soybeans. Yet other cultures, most notably China and Japan, have included this wonderful legume in their diets for over 5,000 years. Unfortunately, we grow soybeans intended for animals and unpalatable to people; those grown for human consumption are processed in every imaginable fashion, when we could simply cook them up!

Some delicious soybean varieties are available. They grow as easily as the indigestible ones you may already have tried and dismissed.

Lentil Loaf

SERVES 4

1 onion, chopped

2 cloves garlic, chopped

1/4 cauliflower, broken into small florets

1 small parsnip, chopped

2 carrots, chopped

3 Tbsp oil

1 1/2 cups dried lentils, cooked until tender with a bay leaf

1 egg, beaten

1 cup bread crumbs or cooked grain

1 tsp curry powder or dry mustard

tomato sauce (optional)

❖ Sauté vegetables in oil until tender-crisp. Preheat oven to 300°F.

Combine all ingredients except tomato sauce and form into a loaf. Add a little water or stock if mixture seems too heavy. Bake in a greased baking pan for about 2 hours. Serve with tomato sauce, if desired.

Lentil Burgers

SERVES 4

2 cups cooked lentils

1 cup whole wheat bread crumbs

1/2 cup wheat germ

1/2 tsp salt

1/2 onion, grated

1/2 tsp celery seeds

whole wheat flour

3 Tbsp oil

❖ Mash lentils lightly. Add bread crumbs, wheat germ, salt, onion and celery seeds. Mix well. Form the mixture into 8 patties. Coat with flour. Heat the oil in a skillet and fry the patties on both sides until browned. Serve as is, or in burger buns with your favourite garnishes.

Sound Nutrition

Many people are worried about getting enough protein, yet our protein needs have been greatly exaggerated. The average American consumes 90 to 120 grams per day, when the US government-recommended intake is between 20 and 40 grams a day.

Chick-peas have been grown in Mediterranean countries since as early as 8,000 BC. The Romans used the word arietnum ("ram-like") to describe this bean because the roundish, compressed seed of some varieties resembles a ram's head with horns curling over the sides. Cicer arietnum was a staple of their diet and still plays an important part in the regional cooking of southern Europe. Chick-peas are widely grown in India and Burma where they rival wheat in acreage under cultivation and are India's most important legume.

Chick-pea Loaf

SERVES 6

3 cups cooked chick-peas

1 cup chopped celery

¹/₄ cup finely chopped onion

1 cup whole wheat bread crumbs

¹/₃ cup tomato sauce

1 Tbsp soy sauce

2 Tbsp soy or whole wheat flour

1 cup finely chopped nuts (walnuts, almonds, cashews)

1 tsp dried sage

2 Tbsp oil

2 Tbsp chopped fresh parsley

2 eggs, lightly beaten

salt to taste

❖ Preheat oven to 375°F. Mash the chick-peas and put in a large bowl. Add all other ingredients and mix well. Turn into a well-oiled loaf pan and bake 30 minutes until set.

Wheatberry Casserole

SERVES 6–8

We like butternut squash in this recipe.

2¹/₂ cups cubed and peeled squash

1 cup sliced carrot

2 cups cooked wheatberries

2 Tbsp chopped chives or scallions

1 Tbsp soy sauce

**2 cups shredded cheddar
or Monterey jack cheese**

❖ Steam squash and carrots for 15 minutes. In a large casserole, toss cooked squash and carrots with wheatberries, chives and soy sauce. Sprinkle with cheese and broil 5 minutes or until cheese is melted and browned.

Alternately, prepare casserole in advance and bake at 375°F. until cheese is melted and vegetable mixture is heated through.

Grower's Delight

Amaranth is among the most stunning, vital plants in the garden. It is exceptionally hardy, grows in the driest of climates and requires virtually no cultivation. Purple amaranth has deep purple leaves and flamboyant seed heads that are eye-catchers wherever they grow.

Amaranth Carrot Loaf

SERVES 6

1 1/2 cups cooked amaranth

1 1/2 cups cooked brown rice

1/2 cup bread crumbs

1 cup sliced mushrooms

1 cup grated carrot

1 cup grated aged cheddar cheese

1 large onion, chopped

2 cloves garlic, minced

2 tsp soy sauce

1/8 tsp cayenne pepper

4 large eggs

❖ Preheat oven to 325°F. In a large bowl, combine all the ingredients but the eggs and mix well. In a separate bowl, beat the eggs, then add to the other ingredients and stir. Turn into a 9–10" square baking casserole or two loaf pans. Bake 45–50 minutes, till set.

Greens and Grains Casserole

SERVES 5–6

1 cup grated cheddar cheese

1 Tbsp butter

2 cups hot cooked amaranth or quinoa

2 Tbsp chopped leek or onion

1 tsp salt

2 Tbsp minced fresh parsley

1 cup steamed young amaranth or quinoa greens

1¹/₂ cups milk

2 eggs, slightly beaten

❖ Preheat oven to 325°F. Stir cheese and butter into hot grain. Add leek, salt, parsley and greens. Stir milk into slightly beaten eggs. Combine with grain mixture. Pour into oiled casserole. Bake until set, about 35 minutes.

Grower's Delight

Amaranth has been known to yield almost 20 tons of greens per acre.

Baked Squash and Quinoa

SERVES 4–6

2 cups coarsely shredded zucchini or other squash

2 Tbsp butter or oil

2 cups cooked quinoa

2 cups grated cheddar cheese

salt and pepper to taste

❖ In a large skillet, cook squash in butter over medium-high heat until softened. Stir in quinoa, cheese and seasoning to taste. Place in greased casserole and bake 30 minutes.

Substantial Sides

Our country lives are full and diverse, which means time for cooking can be limited. Sometimes we find it more convenient to snack through the day. Many of these "side" dishes make fine lunches or light dinners. They definitely don't scrimp on nutrition!

Sometimes our simplest meals are the most nourishing in an unusual kind of way. Thinking of all the millions of people who subsist on basic grain and water from day to day, makes us appreciate the abundance of our food and the diversity of our diet.

Thich Nhat Hanh, who teaches mindful living, has this to say: "Having the opportunity to sit with our family and friends and enjoy wonderful food is something precious, something not everyone has. Many people in the world are hungry. When I hold a bowl of rice or a piece of bread, I know that I am fortunate, and I feel compassion for all those who have no food to eat and are without friends or family. This is a very deep practice. We do not need to go to a temple or a church in order to practice this. We can practice it right at our dinner table. Mindful eating can cultivate seeds of compassion and understanding that will strengthen us to do something to help hungry and lonely people be nourished."

The Recipes

Grower's Delight

One of our favourite varieties of lentil has a delicate blue flower and large triangular seed. We think it deserves a more appealing name than Horse Lentil!

Carlos Beca's Lentils

SERVES 3–4

A snap of fresh ginger gives this recipe extra oomph for a cold winter's day.

1 onion, chopped

1 clove garlic, chopped

2 Tbsp oil

1 tsp curry powder

¹/₂ tsp ground cumin

1 cup dried lentils

2–3 cups water

1 tsp salt

1 Tbsp freshly grated ginger (optional)

❖ Sauté the onion and garlic in oil. Add the curry and cumin and sauté 1 minute longer. Add a little water if too dry. Add the lentils and 2–3 cups of water depending on how much sauce you like. Add the salt and ginger, if desired. Bring to a boil and cook over very low heat for 20–30 minutes.

BarleyBeanBravo

SERVES 6

1 onion, chopped

1 cup chopped sweet pepper (green, red or a combination)

2 Tbsp oil

1¹/₃ cups water

1 cup salsa or taco sauce

¹/₂ tsp ground cumin

¹/₄ tsp dried oregano

¹/₂ cup barley

1 cup cooked pinto or kidney beans

❖ Sauté onion and pepper in oil in a large saucepan until softened. Stir in water, salsa, cumin and oregano and bring to boil. Stir in barley and return to boiling. Cover and simmer 40–50 minutes. Stir in beans. Simmer a few minutes longer or until beans are heated through.

Grower's Delight

Most barley varieties have long, colourful awns that please the eye and enchant the ear when blown by summer breezes. For a really delightful effect, try planting golden-tinged varieties, like Ethiopian, near bronze or reddish-tinged ones, such as Excelsior.

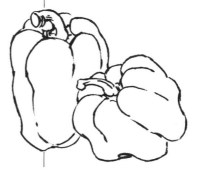

Though peas contain average amounts of minerals compared to other legumes, they are rich in the B vitamins thiamine, riboflavin and niacin, and contain a small amount of vitamin A.

Barley or Wheat with Peas

SERVES 4

1 cup fresh or frozen peas

2 Tbsp finely chopped scallion, garlic greens or chives

1 Tbsp butter

2 cups cooked whole wheat or barley

1/2 tsp salt

❖ Stir peas, scallions and butter into the cooking grain just before it is done. Cover and simmer 5 more minutes or until the peas are heated through. Add salt to taste.

Barley or Wheat with Pasta

SERVES 4–6

1 cup chopped onion

2 Tbsp oil

4 cups finely chopped cabbage

1 Tbsp butter

1 cup cooked whole wheat or barley

1/2 cup cooked bow ties or other small pasta

3/4 tsp salt

1/2 tsp pepper

❖ In a large skillet, sauté the onion in oil until golden. Add cabbage and continue to cook, stirring until wilted. Add butter, then stir in barley, pasta, salt and pepper. Continue stirring until barley and pasta are heated through.

Did You Know . . . ?

Barley was first grown in ancient Egypt, and was a staple bread grain of the Greeks and Romans. In Europe, its use as a bread grain pre-dates wheat and rye, which ultimately replaced it.

Grower's Delight

In the garden, kamut is one of the most eye-catching of wheat strains. Although it predates modern wheats, its seed head and kernels are twice the size of normal wheat. There is a noticeable "gooseneck" at the top of each stem.

Barley, Leek and Lentil Lift

SERVES 4–6

3 cups finely chopped leeks

2 Tbsp oil

2³/₄ cups stock or water

³/₄ cup dried lentils

¹/₂ cup barley

1 bay leaf

¹/₂ tsp dried rosemary

salt and soy sauce to taste

❖ Sauté leeks in oil in a large saucepan on medium-high heat until softened. Add stock and bring to boil. Stir in lentils, barley, bay leaf and rosemary. Cover and simmer 50 minutes or until liquid has been absorbed. Season. Remove bay leaf.

Barley Pilaf

SERVES 4

1 cup barley

2²/₃ cups Vegetable Stock

1 onion, sliced

1 celery stalk, finely chopped

2 Tbsp oil

2 cups mushrooms, sliced

¹/₄ tsp dried thyme

1 Tbsp soy sauce

salt to taste

❖ Simmer the barley and stock in a covered pot for 1 hour. Sauté the onion and celery in oil for about 5 minutes. Add the mushrooms and thyme, then sauté until the onion and celery are transparent and the mushrooms are slightly soft. Combine with the cooked barley and simmer the pilaf 5–10 minutes longer, or until the liquid is absorbed and the flavours blended. Season with soy sauce and salt.

Variation: Instead of mushrooms, add other vegetables such as carrots, parsnips, peppers, zucchini or squash. Vary sautéing time accordingly or add a bit of water to steam. Top with toasted pumpkin or sunflower seeds.

Did You Know . . . ?

According to ancient Central American lore, grains help foster socialization and social interaction. In the West, breaking bread with others is considered the ultimate symbol of close relations.

Stuffed Zucchini with Amaranth or Quinoa

SERVES 5–6

1 large zucchini

4 Tbsp butter

1 onion, chopped

1 celery stalk, chopped

1 green or red sweet pepper, chopped

1 cup sliced mushrooms

1 tsp Spike or other vegetable seasoning

3–4 cloves garlic, minced

¹/₂ cup chopped almonds or walnuts

1¹/₂ cups cooked amaranth or quinoa

¹/₂ cup grated cheddar cheese

❖ Preheat oven to 325°F. Cut the zucchini in half lengthwise. Scoop out the flesh and chop it. Sauté the zucchini chunks in butter with the other vegetables, Spike and garlic. Combine nuts and amaranth with vegetables. Stuff into zucchini. Bake 30 minutes. Sprinkle cheese on top and bake 5 minutes longer.

Curried Quinoa

SERVES 6

¹/₄ cup butter
1 onion, chopped
2 cloves garlic, chopped
1 tsp grated ginger
1 Tbsp curry powder
¹/₂ tsp ground coriander
¹/₂ tsp salt
¹/₄ tsp turmeric
¹/₄ tsp ground cumin
¹/₈ tsp cayenne
1 cup fresh peas
1¹/₄ cups Vegetable Stock
¹/₂ cup quinoa

❖ In a large saucepan, melt butter over medium-high heat. Add onion, garlic and ginger. Cook, stirring frequently, until onion softens. Stir in spices and cook for 1 minute or until absorbed. Stir in peas and stock. Cover and simmer 5 minutes. Add quinoa or amaranth and return to boiling. Cover and simmer 15 minutes longer or until liquid has been absorbed.

Variation: Substitute amaranth for the quinoa.

Sound Nutrition

Quinoa's simple, distinctive taste makes it extremely versatile. It can be substituted for almost any grain in virtually any recipe. Because it's not a true cereal grain, people who suffer from cereal grain allergies can take special advantage of this versatility.

It's hard to believe that a tiny amaranth seed can produce a plant with a trunk-like stalk that is taller than a person in three or four months. Or that that same seed will yield as many as 50,000 seeds for planting next year!

Amaranth with Leeks and Asparagus

SERVES 4–6

1 cup sliced leeks

2 Tbsp oil

1 cup asparagus pieces and tips

1 cup amaranth

❖ Sauté leeks in oil over medium-high heat until soft. In the meantime, cook asparagus and amaranth separately. Stir all together.

Sautéed Amaranth Greens

SERVES 4

2 cloves garlic, finely chopped

1 onion, sliced

1 green pepper, chopped

1 Tbsp oil

4 cups amaranth greens

1 cup mung bean, adzuki, alfalfa or other sprouts

1 Tbsp soy sauce

1 Tbsp water

❖ Stir-fry garlic, onion and green pepper in oil in a heavy skillet for 3–5 minutes. Stir in greens and sprouts. Mix soy sauce and water, then add to vegetables. Cover and cook over medium heat 4–5 minutes.

Variation: Kale or quinoa greens are good substitutes for amaranth greens.

Soul Food

"Besides having edible leaves and providing an extremely nutritious grain from its huge seed heads, amaranth is a spectacularly beautiful plant—extraordinarily colorful. I call it a movie star of a plant. It is simply the most beautiful crop plant possible. And wherever it grows in the world, it is also involved in the mysticism and the religion of the people, as well . . . Amaranth is not just a thing to eat, it is a thing of the spirit."

— Robert Rodale, *Save Three Lives*

Humans have eaten garlic for at least 10,000 years. In fact, a garlic shortage caused the first recorded labour strike by slaves during the building of the pyramids in Egypt.

Garlic Pasta

SERVES 4

1 pound dried pasta (any kind)

1–2 garlic bulbs, separated into cloves, peeled and chopped

1 large onion, finely chopped

1/4 cup olive oil

salt and pepper to taste

grated cheese or nutritional yeast (optional)

❖ Prepare the pasta al dente. While the pasta is cooking, sauté the garlic and onion in the olive oil. Cook over medium heat, easing the flavour out and being careful not to brown. When the pasta is ready, drain it and put it in a large bowl. Pour the garlic, onion and oil over it. Add pepper and a little salt. Toss well until all the pasta is glistening. Serve immediately.

Sprinkle with grated cheese or nutritional yeast, if desired.

Festive Fare

For many people, good intentions fall to pieces in the face of tradition. "That's what I've always had for Christmas. That's what I'll always have!"

Last Christmas season we enjoyed the most wonderful festive spread we ever had—without turkey and dressing. Whatever your festive food choices, we hope you'll find a few here to brighten up your banquet table. And while you have the opportunity to share a wonderful repast with family and friends, you may be inspired to offer a ritual acknowledgement for the food, the energies through which it came to your table, and a blessing on the company . . .

We give thanks for this food that is laid
    before us
And for all things in the web of life that
    have brought it to our table:
  The soil, the rain, the wind, the sun;
  The hands that have tended it, and
  The hands that have prepared it lovingly
    for our nourishment.
We give thanks for family and friends who
    come together in celebration.
May this food nourish our bodies, sustain
    our hearts, and empower our sense of
    Oneness with all Life.

The Recipes

Martha Warde's Five-Bean Salad

SERVES 8–10

³/₄ cup fresh green beans, steamed

³/₄ cup fresh yellow beans, steamed

³/₄ cup cooked red kidney beans

³/₄ cup cooked lima beans

³/₄ cup cooked chick-peas

1 green or red sweet pepper, diced

1 large red or yellow sweet onion, sliced thin

¹/₂ cup brown sugar

¹/₂ cup red wine vinegar

¹/₂ cup olive oil

¹/₂ tsp dry mustard

¹/₂ tsp finely chopped fresh tarragon

¹/₂ tsp finely chopped fresh basil

2 Tbsp chopped fresh parsley

❖ Mix beans, pepper and onion in a large bowl. Combine remaining ingredients and drizzle over vegetables. Cover and marinate for several hours or overnight, stirring once or twice. Before serving, stir and drain. The flavour improves as it stands.

Mixed Bean Salad

SERVES 8

1/2 cup dried black beans

*1/2 cup dried two-tone beans
(Aunt Jean, Wild Goose or pinto)*

1 cup dried kidney beans

1 1/2 cups sliced green beans

2 cups sliced mushrooms

2 Tbsp oil

*1 small onion, finely chopped, or 1/2 cup
chopped shallots*

1/4 cup minced fresh parsley

2 cloves garlic, pressed or finely chopped

1/3 cup cider vinegar

1/3 cup olive oil

2 Tbsp honey

1/2 tsp salt

pepper to taste

❖ Soak and cook the dried beans separately. Steam the green beans unttil tender-crisp. Sauté the mushrooms in the 2 Tbsp oil. Blend the onion, parsley, garlic, vinegar, olive oil, honey, salt and pepper. Mix and toss all ingredients and marinate at least 1 hour before serving.

Soul Food

"For our healing we have on our side one great force: the power of Creation, with good care, with kindly use, to heal itself."
— Wendell Berry, *The Unsettling of America*

Oriental Quinoa Salad

SERVES 6

3 cups cooked quinoa

3 scallions, sliced

³/4 cup thinly sliced bok choy

3 Tbsp sesame seeds, toasted

¹/4 cup slivered almonds, toasted

¹/2 cup sliced mushrooms

¹/4 cup diagonally sliced celery

¹/4 cup bean sprouts

Dressing:

¹/4 cup olive oil

3 Tbsp soy sauce

2 Tbsp fresh lemon juice

1 Tbsp brown sugar

1 tsp grated ginger

❖ Combine salad ingredients. Combine dressing ingredients. Toss together.

Minestrone for 10

SERVES 10

1 large onion, chopped

1 Tbsp oil

2 cloves garlic, chopped

7 cups stock

1 carrot, cubed or sliced

2 potatoes, cubed

1 tomato, cubed

1/2 cup fresh green beans, chopped to match other veggies

1 tsp each salt, dried sage, dried parsley, dried oregano

1/2 cup greens (amaranth, quinoa, spinach)

1/2 cup small shell pasta, cooked a bit firmer than al dente

1/2 cup dried white beans, soaked and cooked

freshly grated Parmesan cheese (optional)

Beans are a boon to diabetics, hypoglycemics and those on weight-loss diets. For one, they retain water in the digestive tract, which promotes a feeling of fullness and delays the return of hunger. In addition, only 2 to 6 percent of the calories in beans are derived from fat, in contrast to 75 to 85 percent for meat and cheese. The only exception is soybeans, which have 34 percent fat calories. As with all beans, though, the fat is polyunsaturated and less harmful than the fat in animal products. Beans are cholesterol-free, and recent research shows that they even contain a chemical that fights the deposit of fat globules in veins and arteries. Not only do they control blood cholesterol, they also control glucose. Unlike other carbohydrate foods, such as bread, cereals, potatoes and pasta, beans don't trigger a rise in blood sugar or require that the pancreas pour out extra insulin to readjust the glucose level in the blood.

❖ In a large pot, sauté onion in oil for 5 minutes. Add garlic and sauté 2 minutes longer. Add stock and bring to a boil. Add carrots and cook 5 minutes. Add potatoes, tomato, green beans and seasonings, and simmer until vegetables are tender. Add greens, beans and pasta. Lower heat and simmer until pasta is done. Sprinkle with grated Parmesan, if desired.

Fruity Lentil Salad

SERVES 6

2 cups dried lentils

1–2 oranges, peeled and sectioned

3 Tbsp fresh lime juice

1/4–1/2 tsp each grated orange and lemon rind

1 small carrot, grated

1/4 large red onion, finely minced

1/2 cup packed currants or raisins

1 large clove garlic, crushed

3 Tbsp cider vinegar

4 Tbsp olive oil

1/2 tsp salt

1/2 cup each finely chopped red and yellow sweet pepper

a handful each of finely chopped fresh parsley, chives and mint

❖ Cook the lentils, drain them and rinse in cold water. Add the remaining ingredients except the sweet pepper and fresh herbs, cover tightly, and chill at least 4 hours. Stir in the pepper and herbs no more than 1 hour before serving.

Soul Food

"Never underestimate the impact of single individuals, working sincerely to create health, understanding, and peace in their own lives. For every step we take to establish genuinely healthy food choices is a step into our own wholeness, into the power to create healthy lives for ourselves, and to contribute to the health and well-being of others."

—John Robbins, Diet for a New World

Garlic Bread

SERVES 4–6

1 loaf French or Italian bread

8 Tbsp butter, softened

3–6 cloves garlic, pressed

$1/3$ cup freshly grated Parmesan cheese

2 tsp minced fresh oregano

❖ Preheat oven to 350°F. Cut bread into slices. Mash together the butter and pressed garlic and blend in the cheese and oregano. Spread mixture on both sides of each slice, wrap loaf lightly in foil and bake 20 minutes. Serve hot.

Enchiladas

SERVES 6–8

2–3 Tbsp oil

1¹/₂ cups chopped onion

2 cups stewed tomatoes

1 cup tomato sauce

2 cloves garlic, minced

pinch cayenne pepper

hot sauce to taste

¹/₂ Tbsp plus 1 tsp chili powder

1 Tbsp honey

¹/₂ tsp ground cumin

*1¹/₂ cups black olives, pitted and sliced
(reserve some for garnish)*

1¹/₂ cups cooked pinto beans, mashed

8 soft corn tortillas

1 cup grated cheddar or other cheese

❖ Heat half the oil and sauté 1 cup of the onion until translucent. Add tomatoes, tomato sauce, half the garlic, the cayenne, hot sauce, ¹/₂ Tbsp chili powder, honey and cumin. Simmer, uncovered, for 20 minutes.

Heat remaining oil and sauté remaining onions, garlic and the olives until onions are translucent. Add remaining 1 tsp chili plus

Food for Thought

"Of special significance is the responsibility that we bear toward our children. We hold their world in sacred trust. What we do to the world around us, we do to them. Our prodigal living is their deprivation. None of the generations that come after us will ever see any of the species that we extinguish. There is a single earthly heritage for everyone on the earth and for all the generations that will ever be. The fluorescence of the planet that we protect and enhance is beyond question the most sublime gift that we can bestow upon them."

— Thomas Berry, in
The Green Lifestyle Handbook

the beans. Stir well and add a little sauce if mix seems too sticky.

Preheat oven to 350°F. Fill each tortilla with 2–3 Tbsp filling and 1 Tbsp grated cheese. Roll up and put in a shallow baking pan. Cover with sauce, sprinkle with remaining cheese and garnish with reserved olives. Bake until bubbling hot, about 30 minutes.

Baked Beans for 25

SERVES 25

4 cups dried beans, soaked (pinto, kidney, navy)

2 cups chopped tomato

4 medium onions, chopped

6 cloves garlic, chopped

6 green or red sweet peppers, chopped

¹/₂ cup tomato paste

¹/₂ cup oil

³/₄ cup miso or bean cooking liquid

¹/₄ cup cider or red wine vinegar

2¹/₂ Tbsp paprika

1¹/₂ Tbsp grated fresh ginger

1 Tbsp ground cumin

2 tsp cayenne pepper

❖ Preheat oven to 350°F. Mix beans, tomatoes, onions, garlic and green pepper and place in a large baking tray. Mix all remaining ingredients together and stir them into the beans and vegetables. Cover and bake 2 hours. If there is not enough liquid from the tomatoes, add some water or stock.

Soybeans for 50

SERVES 50

12 cups soybeans

8 leeks, chopped

1 Tbsp grated fresh ginger

ground cumin, Spike, Vegit, or other seasoning to taste

¹/₃ cup butter

¹/₂ cup bean cooking liquid or miso

1 cup molasses

¹/₂ cup chopped fresh Italian parsley

❖ Cook soybeans. In a large pot, cook leeks, ginger and cumin in butter until leeks are golden. Add remaining ingredients except parsley and simmer on stove top for 20 minutes, or bake in a 350°F oven for 30 minutes. Add chopped parsley near the end.

Mayan Stew

SERVES 6

1 tsp ground cumin

1 tsp dried oregano

1 tsp coriander seeds

1 tsp nutmeg

¹/₂ tsp cinnamon

3 whole cloves

2 tsp chili powder or 3 dried chilies, chopped

1 Tbsp paprika

4 Tbsp olive oil

1 large onion, chopped

2 cloves garlic, finely chopped

1 tsp salt

3 cups cooked pinto beans, bean cooking liquid reserved

4 cups pumpkin or winter squash, cubed

6 tomatoes, chopped

1¹/₂ cups corn kernels (about 3 ears)

1 Tbsp chopped cilantro, or to taste

❖ Pulverize unground seasonings with a mortar and pestle or in a spice grinder.

Heat the oil in a large skillet and sauté onion over high heat for 1 minute. Lower heat to medium and add the garlic, spices and seasonings. Combine well, then add ½ cup of the reserved bean broth. Cook until the onion is soft.

Add the pumpkin and cook about 20 minutes. Add the tomatoes, corn and beans. Cook 20 minutes longer or until the pumpkin is tender. Add more bean liquid if necessary to keep all ingredients covered.

Serve in bowls, garnished with chopped cilantro.

Chana Masaledar

SERVES 4

2 Tbsp oil

¹/₄ tsp whole cumin seeds

1 medium onion, chopped

1 tsp ground coriander

¹/₄ tsp each cinnamon, nutmeg and cloves

2 cloves garlic, chopped fine

¹/₂ tsp grated fresh ginger

1 Tbsp tomato paste

2¹/₂ cups cooked chick-peas

4 Tbsp water, or more as needed

¹/₂ tsp salt

pinch cayenne pepper

1 Tbsp fresh lemon juice

Garnish:

1 firm tomato, cut into eighths

¹/₂ medium onion, cut into coarse slivers

4 long slices green pepper

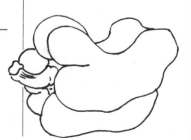

❖ Heat oil in a heavy skillet over medium-high heat. Add cumin seeds, and as soon as they start to darken, add the chopped onion. Fry 7–8 minutes, stirring frequently, until onions begin to turn golden brown.

Turn heat to low and mix in coriander, cinnamon, nutmeg and cloves. Add garlic and ginger and cook, stirring, 2–3 minutes.

Add tomato paste, chick-peas, 4 Tbsp water, salt, cayenne and lemon juice to pan. Mix well. Cover and simmer over medium-low heat for about 10 minutes, gently stirring occasionally. Add more water, a tablespoon at a time, if mixture seems dry.

Serve in bowls and line the edges with tomato, onion and green pepper garnishes.

Mung Beans with Capers and Lemon

SERVES 6

This, our only mung bean recipe, is delectable! The zesty lemon and caper combination makes it a tasty side dish in any meal—vegetarian, fish or meat.

1 cup dried mung beans

2 Tbsp oil

2 medium onions, finely chopped

2 cloves garlic, minced

2 Tbsp capers

juice and grated rind of 1 large lemon

¹/₄ cup chopped fresh parsley

❖ Soak mung beans for about an hour, then cook in fresh water for 40 minutes or until done. Drain.

Heat the oil over medium-low heat in a saucepan or skillet. Add the onions and garlic and cook till soft. Stir in the beans, capers, rind and lemon juice. Cover and simmer 2 minutes. Add the parsley or use as a garnish, and serve.

Sound Nutrition

Barley provides good quantities of minerals, especially potassium, iron, phosphorus and calcium.

Barley with Toasted Almonds

SERVES 2–3

2¹/₂ cups Vegetable Stock

1 cup barley

¹/₂ cup almonds

¹/₃ cup chopped fresh chervil or parsley

pepper to taste

❖ Bring the stock to a boil in medium saucepan. Add barley and cook 50 minutes or until liquid has been absorbed.

Meanwhile, toast the almonds for 10 minutes on a baking sheet in a 350°F oven, or in a skillet over medium-high heat, stirring occasionally.

When the barley is cooked, toss with the almonds, chervil and pepper.

Squash with Chick-pea Stuffing

SERVES 2

¹/₄ cup dried chick-peas

1 squash, zucchini or eggplant

¹/₄ cup cooked brown rice

1 onion, chopped

1 tomato, chopped

salt and pepper to taste

1 tsp fresh lemon juice

¹/₂ tsp ground allspice

❖ Soak chick-peas. Cook well and mash. Preheat oven to 350°F. Cut squash in half lengthwise and scoop out flesh, leaving ¹/₄″ layer on the shell. (Reserve for another use.) Combine chick-peas, rice, onion, tomato, salt, pepper, lemon juice and allspice. Fill squash halves. Place in ovenproof dish, cover and bake 50 minutes or until vegetables are tender.

Sound Nutrition

Many studies have reported consistent findings regarding major diseases such as cancer, diabetes and heart disease. Risks are much lower with fat levels at about 10-15 percent of daily intake and with cholesterol eliminated or drastically reduced.

Zucchini with Amaranth Stuffing

SERVES 5–6

1 large zucchini or squash

1 onion, chopped

1 celery stalk, chopped

1 green or red sweet pepper, chopped

1 cup sliced mushrooms

1 tsp Spike or other vegetable seasoning

3–4 cloves garlic, minced

4 Tbsp butter

1 1/2 cups cooked amaranth

1/2 cup chopped almonds or walnuts

1/2 cup grated cheddar cheese

❖ Preheat oven to 325°F. Cut zucchini in half lengthwise and scoop out flesh, leaving 1/4" layer on the shell. (Reserve for another use.) Sauté onion, celery, green pepper, mushrooms, Spike and garlic in butter. Combine with amaranth and nuts. Fill zucchini halves. Bake 30 minutes. Sprinkle cheese on top and bake 5 minutes longer.

Variation: Substitute quinoa for the amaranth.

Lima Beans Deluxe

SERVES 4

The combined flavours of pineapple, cheese and beans make this an unusual side for a pot luck feast. It gets rave reviews.

2/3 cup dried lima beans, soaked

---

2 Tbsp oil

---

1 large green pepper, diced

---

2 stalks celery, diced

---

1 onion, chopped

---

2 cloves garlic, finely chopped

---

1 tsp salt

---

1 1/2 Tbsp sesame seeds, toasted (optional)

1/2 cup pineapple tidbits

---

1 1/2 cups soup stock (optional)

---

1 1/2 cups grated cheddar cheese

❖ Cook the beans till tender. Drain and reserve the cooking liquid.

Preheat oven to 375°F. Heat the oil and sauté the green pepper, celery, onion and garlic 10 minutes or until tender. Combine cooked ingredients with the beans, salt, seeds, fruit and the stock or reserved bean liquid. Mix the ingredients well, then add half the cheese.

Grower's Delight

One of the most gorgeous lima beans is also one of the most delicious. Christmas Lima is a large white and maroon bean with a pecan-like flavour.

Turn the mixture into an oiled 1-quart casserole and bake 25 minutes. Increase oven temperature to 400°F, top casserole with the remaining cheese and bake 10–15 minutes longer to form a crust.

Variation: Substitute raisins for the pineapple.

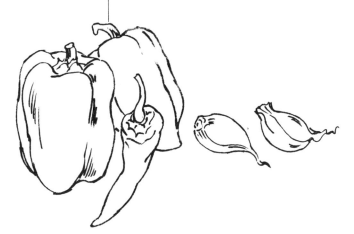

Sources

Most of our comments come from a combination of experience, conversations with others, and bits and pieces we "sift" from the slew of articles, books and magazines that cross our paths. For more information on the implications of food choices, and for organic and sustainable gardening information, we recommend Dan's book, *Greening the Garden*.

The statistical information under **Did You Know...?** and **Sound Nutrition** comes from:

Atlas, Nava. *The Wholefood Catalog: A Complete Guide to Natural Foods*. New York: Fawcett Columbine, 1988.

Colbin, Annemarie. *Food and Healing*. New York: Random House, 1986.

Context Institute (Bainbridge Island WA). "Facts Out of Context" columns, *In Context*, vols. 24, 29, 30, 32.

Klaper, Michael. *Vegan Nutrition: Pure and Simple*. Umatilla FL: Gentle World Inc., 1987.

Robbins, John. *Diet for a New America*. Walpole NH: Stillpoint Publishing, 1987.

_____. *Diet for a New World*. New York: Avon, 1992.

Vegetarian Resource Group (Baltimore). *Vegetarian Journal*, July/August 1994.

Quotations cited in the text and in **Grower's Delight, Soul Food** and **Food for Thought** are taken from:

Anderson, Edgar. *Plants, Man and Life*. Berkeley: University of California Press, 1952.

Ausubel, Kenny. *Seeds of Change: The Living Treasure*. San Francisco: Harper, 1994.

Berry, Thomas. *The Dream of the Earth*. San Francisco: Sierra Club, 1988.

Berry, Wendell. *The Unsettling of America: Culture and Agriculture*. San Francisco: Sierra Club, 1977.

_____. *What Are People For?* (essays). San Francisco: North Point, 1990.

The Bible. Isaiah 5:8.

Deppe, Carol. *Breed Your Own Vegetable Varieties*. Boston: Little, Brown, 1993.

Duesing, Bill. *Living on the Earth*. East Haven: Long River Books, 1993.

Fowler, Cary and Pat Mooney. *Shattering: Food, Politics and the Loss of Genetic Diversity*. Tucson: University of Arizona Press, 1990.

Gibran, Kahlil. *The Prophet*. New York: Knopf, 1971.

Johnson, Lorraine. *Green Future: How to Make a World of Difference*. Markahm ON: Penguin, 1990.

Kneen, Brewster. *From Land to Mouth: Understanding the Food System*. Toronto: NC Press, 1993.

Nearing, Helen. *Simple Food for the Good Life: An Alternative Cook Book*. New York: Dell, 1980.

Rifkin, Jeremy, ed. *The Green Lifestyle Handbook: 1001 Ways You Can Heal the Earth*. Markham ON: Fitzhenry & Whiteside, 1990.

Robbins, John. *Diet for a New World*. New York: Avon, 1992.

Rodale, Robert. *Save Three Lives: A Plan for Famine Prevention*. San Francisco: Sierra Club, 1991.

Did you know . . . ?

The current scale of and approach to cattle breeding by modern agribusiness has had these effects, among others:

- *a small-scale, hundred-head dairy operation generates as much pollution as a town with 2,000 citizens;*

- *85 percent of topsoil loss in North America is directly associated with raising livestock;*

- *half of all the water consumed in North America goes to irrigate land that supports feed and fodder for livestock;*

- *cows annually add more than 50 million tons of methane into the atmosphere and constitute one of the largest contributors to the greenhouse effect;*

- *animal agriculture is the greatest producer of both methane, which contributes to the greenhouse effect, and sewage waste —over 2 billion tons of manure each year, estimated at ten times that of humans.*

Helpful Resources and Further Reading

For compelling reading, we can recommend any of the publications listed in the Sources section above. Here are some additional contacts and resources, which we know from first-hand experience or from the recommendations of valued colleagues.

Beans and Grains

Contacts

The Aprovecho Institute (re: favas)
80574 Hazelton Road
Cottage Grove OR 97424
USA

Chick-pea Project
Carol Deppe
Box 471
Corvallis OR 97330-0471
USA

Cookbooks

Gelles, Carol. *The Complete Whole Grain Cookbook*. New York: Donald L. Fine, 1989.

Spicer, Kay and Violet Currie. *Full of Beans*. Campbellville ON: Mighton House, 1993.

Stone, Sally and Martin. *The Brilliant Bean*. New York: Bantam, 1977.

Plant-based Diet

All of these cookbooks contain lots of information and suggestions along with the recipes.

Levitt, Jo Ann, et al. *Kripalu Kitchen: A Natural Foods Cookbook and Nutritional Guide.* Lennox MA: Kripalu Publications, 1980.

Robbins, John. *Diet for a New World.* New York: Avon, 1992.

Robertson, Laurel, et al. *Laurel's Kitchen.* New York: Bantam, 1976.

Tracy, Lisa. *The Gradual Vegetarian: For Everyone Finally Ready to Make the Change.* New York: M. Evans and Co., 1985.

Food and Health

Carroll, Mary and Hal Straus. *The No Cholesterol Cookbook.* Pennsylvania: Rodale, 1991.

Colbin, Annemarie. *Food and Healing.* New York: Random House, 1986.

Matsen, Jonn. *Eating Alive: Prevention Thru Good Digestion.* Vancouver: Crompton Books, 1987.

Pollution Probe Foundation. *Additive Alert! What Have They Done to Our Food? A Consumer's Action Guide.* Toronto: McClelland and Stewart, 1994.

Food Choices for Sustainability

Jason, Dan. *Greening the Garden: A Guide to Sustainable Growing.* Philadelphia: New Society, 1991.

Lappé, Frances Moore. *Diet for a Small Planet*. New York: Ballantine, 1982.

Robbins, John. *Diet for a New America*. Walpole NH: Stillpoint Publishing, 1987.

Sustainability

Andruss, Van, et al, eds. *Home! A Bioregional Reader*. Philadelphia: New Society, 1990.

Mâté, Ferenc. *A Reasonable Life: Toward a Simpler, Secure, More Humane Existence.* Albatross Publishing, 1993.

Perhaps the most comprehensive general audience magazine we've seen that offers practical steps and useful insights about how we can create a more humane, sustainable culture, is *In Context*, published quarterly in theme-based issues. For a subscription, contact:

In Context
The Context Institute
PO Box 11470
Bainbridge Island WA 98110
USA

Information Sources for Organic Food

Canadian Organic Growers (COGnition Magazine)
PO Box 6408, Station J
Ottawa ON K2A 3Y6

Canadian Organic Producers Marketing Co-operative
PO Box 2000
Girvin SK S0G 1X0

Centre for Sustainable Agriculture
Box 9, Group 15
Hadashville, MB R0E 0X0

National Organic Farmers Association
RFD 2, Sheldon Rd.
Barre MA 01005
USA

Organic Food Producers Association of
North America
453 Reynolds St.
Oakville ON L6J 3M6

Gardening

Bennett, Jennifer. *The Harrowsmith Northern Gardener*. Camden East ON: Camden House, 1982.

Coleman, Eliot. *The New Organic Grower: A Master's Manual of Tools and Techniques* for the Home and Market Gardener. Post Mills VT: Chelsea Green Publishing, 1989.

Jason, Dan. *Greening the Garden: A Guide to Sustainable Growing*. Philadelphia: New Society, 1991.

Seymour, John. *The Complete Food Garden*. London: Fontana/Collins, 1980.

Also, see the following magazines:
Organic Gardening Magazine
Emmaus PA 18099
USA

Henry Doubleday Research Association
Magazine
Ryton-on-Dunsmore
Coventry, England CV8 3LG

Harrowsmith Country Life
25 Sheppard Ave. W., Ste. 100
North York ON M2N 6S7

or
Ferry Rd.
Charlotte VT 05445
USA

Alternative Agriculture

Agriculture Alternatives
Box 244
University Centre
University of Guelph
Guelph ON N1G 2W1

Ecological Agriculture Projects
Dr. Stuart B. Hill, Director
PO Box 191, Macdonald College
21, 111 Lakeshore Rd.
Ste-Anne de Bellevue PQ H9X 1C0

National Family Farm Coalition
80 F St. NW, #704
Washington DC 20001
USA

Sustainable Agriculture Project
Center for Rural Affairs
104 E. Main, Box 736
Harrington NE 68739
USA

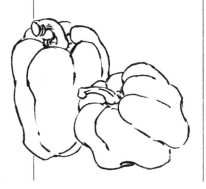

What You Can Do

Food Choices for a Sustainable Household

Individuals making more conscious food choices in their own households can have a powerful impact upon our food systems and the lobbies that protect them. Try some of these ideas for starters!

Make conscious buying decisions.

- Make choices in this order: refuse, reduce, reuse, recycle.

- Reduce the disposable packaging you buy.

- Use large cloth bags or your own bags for grocery purchases.

- Refuse non-recyclable beverage containers.

- Buy the largest quantities of non-perishables possible for budget and storage space available.

- Buy and ask for organic and/or locally grown produce and products.

- Reduce reliance on imported foods, e.g. buy fresh fruits in season, reduce imported fruits through winter, choose products from as close to home as possible.

- Encourage store managers to carry bulk foods, organic foods and products with least packaging possible; praise their efforts.

- Let store managers know why you no longer purchase certain items.

Consider the energy spent in preparing and cooking food.

- Use rags or cloth towels instead of paper.

- Instead of using running water, keep a pan or two of water ready for rinsing hands, wiping up and washing veggies.

- Use cold instead of hot water whenever feasible.

- Use biodegradable dish soaps and other detergents.

- For wipe-ups and cleaning, use hot soapy water, baking soda, vinegar, Borax and cornstarch whenever possible, instead of cleansers, commercial window cleaners or bleach.

- Limit the use of electric appliances and use energy-efficient models.

- Limit the use of the oven and the burners, e.g. have more cold meals in summer and choose "minimum pot" meals.

- Use a pressure cooker instead of conventional pots for energy efficiency.

- Use dishwashers only when full; use energy-saver cycles and let dishes air-dry.

- Avoid keeping refrigerators or freezers too cold (38°F and 5°F respectively should do).

Add another element to the joy of eating.

- Grow some of your own food. A few herbs growing in the kitchen alone will make a difference to the taste of your food!

- Reduce or eliminate processed foods in favour of fresh and whole foods.

- Eat organic, untreated, pesticide-free foods.

- Reduce or eliminate inorganic meats and dairy products in favour of free-range, organic varieties.

- Got a craving? Need something from the fridge? Decide what you want before opening the door. Praise children for doing this!

- Use and reuse cloth napkins at the table. Keep two sets to alternate every few days.

- For large gatherings and picnics, ask guests to bring their own plates, utensils and cups instead of using paper and plastic products.

Food Choices for a Sustainable Community

Groups of individuals can bring about significant changes when inspired by a common, positive vision, motivated by clear intent and empowered by positive attitudes. Here are a few ideas that you, your family, friends, neighbours and interest groups can use to create more sustainable communities.

Expand your buying power as consumers.

- Explore local food co-operatives, buyers' clubs and whole food outlets.

- Plan for, purchase and share the largest quantity of packaged staples and dried bulk foods possible for your budget and storage capabilities.

Get involved in how your food is grown and support low-input, sustainable agriculture.

- Grow items you'd normally buy at the store. Start with a small garden and expand as time and space allow. Make it a family project through which everyone learns together.

- Connect with an organic farmer directly or through organic grower or community-shared agriculture organizations. Arrange to purchase a weekly supply of fresh produce for the next summer on a prepaid basis. This supports small-scale sustainable agriculture, gives your family better nutrition and assures growers a fair and stable income.

- Participate in and learn about community-based farms with family, schoolmates and interest groups.

- Take part in or help start a garden in your community (e.g. parkland or school grounds). Work with others and distribute harvest among workers and/or service organizations such as food banks. Encourage co-operative sharing and learning experiences among social service groups, their

Did You Know . . . ?

It's been said that organic, or "soft technology," methods can reduce energy use by as much as 50 percent over the existing monoculture model.

clients, school classes, etc.

Community Gardens Organizer's Kit
National Gardening Association
180 Flynn Ave.
Burlington VT 05401, USA

- Support restaurants that offer organic produce and vegetarian choices on their menus. Encourage others to do so.

Encourage and support biodiversity.

- Don't use chemical fertilizers on your lawn or garden.

- Transform your lawn into a garden, for either food crops or the beauty of wildlife.

- Urge municipal and provincial or state governments to protect and conserve wilderness areas and agricultural lands and support those who do.

- If you're a gardener, learn about organic growing methods and explore open-pollinated seed sources. Save and exchange seeds with friends or through seed exchanges:

Heritage Seed Program
RR #3
Uxbridge ON L9P 1R3

Seed Savers' Exchange
RR #3, Box 239
Decorah IA 52101, USA

- If you're not a gardener, look into and support local or national organizations that promote organic gardening and sustainable agriculture.

A Guide for Growers

For families interested in becoming protein self-sufficient, growing dried beans is an excellent place to start. And, unless you're at a latitude or an elevation where there are fewer than 100 frost-free days, don't worry about getting dried beans to mature. Beans and grains are a lot easier to grow than ordinary vegetables! As field crops that have been cultivated with minimum inputs for hundreds of years, they are adapted to conditions that don't work very well for lettuce or broccoli. In good garden soil, with only occasional waterings, they can provide many sumptuous meals of nutritious whole food.

We divide our beans and grains into cool and warm weather crops. Wheat, barley, oats, lentils, favas, peas, chick-peas and quinoa will all germinate in fairly cool soil and can be sown in early spring, as soon as the ground can be worked. In places with a mild winter, such as here on the West Coast of BC, most of these crops can be sown in the fall so they can get a head start on spring weeds. Pinto, kidney, turtle and soup beans, as well as limas, adzukis and amaranth, need a warmer temperature to germinate and are best planted around the same time as corn—late May or early June—across the continent.

As a general rule, plant seeds at a depth that is twice their size. However, they can be sown deeper in dry soil, and closer to the surface in wet, heavy soil. To begin with, we recommend planting in rows for easy and efficient management. Thin beans to about 6 inches apart and slightly wider for favas.

Wheat and barley are grasses which we sow about an inch apart and don't thin. Quinoa and amaranth, on the other hand, grow to their full potential if sown 8 to 12 inches apart. Though usually referred to as grains, these South American crops are not true grasses, and they develop into huge plants with thick stalks.

During the growing season, the most important task is to keep the plants moist and as weed-free as possible. Mulching, or covering the soil with straw, leaves or other compostable material, can help enormously in this regard. (In coastal climates, avoid encouraging the slug population by mulching after the peak slug season, when the soil has warmed—usually from June on.) We rarely have to water our beans and grains. They take advantage of soil moisture in spring and early summer to put down deep roots. The most crucial time to maintain adequate soil moisture is when the plants are flowering and setting seed.

All the beans and grains, with the exception of amaranth, should be allowed to dry down completely before they are harvested. The beans get to the point where they rattle in the dry pods. Amaranth is ripe for harvest when rubbing or shaking the seedheads causes seed to fall easily.

We harvest all of these crops by hand, snipping off the heads of wheat, barley, amaranth and quinoa with thumb and forefinger, shears or scissors. Hulls of "hulless" barley and wheat varieties come off easily by hand-rubbing or by stomping on them in a large box. Amaranth and quinoa seeds don't have hulls and can be separated from the seedheads by rubbing through screening into a box or other container. We thresh beans by placing them in a rectangular wooden box and walking or shuffling over them. The shelled pods stay on the surface and can be scooped off.

After initial threshing, separate chaff and seed with a blow-nozzle attached to an air compressor. A fan or hair dryer also works well, as does the use of screening or the traditional method of winnowing in the wind.

Additional drying in a warm protected space will ensure long-term, safe storage. Beans are sufficiently dry when a fingernail cannot dent them. Beans and grains should be stored in airtight containers in a cool, dry place.

All of the beans and grains offered through Salt Spring Seeds are heirloom, or heritage, varieties. Unlike hybrids, these varieties remain true and once grown, seeds may be saved for growing out the following season. So once you find varieties you like, you never have to buy seed again! The other positive aspect of growing heritage over hybrid varieties is that they do not demand chemical pesticides, herbicides or fertilizer.

A number of seed companies are starting to feature heirloom beans and grains. They are sometimes found in local grocery, supermarket or health food stores. And naturally, we'd be happy to send you a Salt Spring Seeds catalogue, which offers a wide selection of beans and grains, plus a sampling of heirloom herb, flower and vegetable seeds.

To receive a Salt Spring Seeds catalogue, send $2.00 with your request to:

Salt Spring Seeds
PO Box 33
Salt Spring Island, BC V0S 1E0, Canada

Index